# MANAGING INFORMATION SYSTEMS

# CONCEPTS & TOOLS

# Managing Information Systems

## Concepts and Tools

Rolland Hurtubise

KUMARIAN PRESS

T
58.6
.H88
1984

Cover design by Marilyn Penrod

Library of Congress Cataloging in Publication Data

Hurtubise, Rolland A., 1942-
  Managing information.

  1. Management information systems. I. Title.
T58.6.H88  1984     658.4'038     84-827
ISBN 0-931816-32-7

The manuscript was written on a Xerox 860 Word-Processing System. The index was composed on an IBM-PC with the Data Base Management System: DBase-II using keywords or instructions available with DBASE-II.

To "common sense" which is not so common.

To those managers anxious to *live* a system design which is more human.

To the information analyst.

Finally, to all of my students and the courses they must *suffer* through.

# TABLE OF CONTENTS

# LIST OF FIGURES

# LIST OF TABLES

# PREFACE

"Do not invent an empire where everything is perfect. For good taste is a virtue which belongs to museum attendants. And if you hold bad taste in contempt, you will have neither painting, nor dance, nor palace, nor garden. You will have become disgusted for fear of the dirty work of the earth. You will thus be deprived by the vacuum of your perfection. Invent an empire where, very simply, everything is fervent."

(Antoine de St-Exupéry,
*Citadelle*, Éditions
Gallimard, Paris, 1948.)

This book is the result of a love affair . . . or if you prefer, an inclination.

For a number of years now, I have wanted to write - in English -a book that would inform the reader on numerous works which span more than fifteen years of professional life. Most of my articles and presentations have been in French, and all of my other books have been written in French. This, my first book in English, is a kind of analysis-synthesis-adaptation of five books published at *Agence d'ARC* in Montréal.

1. INFORMATIQUE ET INFORMATION (Data Processing and Information) 1976,
2. LA GESTION DE L'INFORMATION (The Management of Information) 1978,
3. A LA RECHERCHE DU SIG (In Search of The MIS) 1980,
4. L'ADMINISTRATEUR QUÉBÉCOIS ET LES SYSTÈMES (Systems and the Quebec Administrator) 1981 and
5. L'HUMAIN DANS LE SYSTÈM (The Human Within the System) 1982.

This last is the basis for this book's contents insofar as it depicts my most recent works.

*Managing Information Systems: Concepts and Tools* could be subtitled "The Humanization of Information Systems Design." It is an attempt to illustrate—within the realm of the possible—the *human* considerations related to the design of *Management Information Systems, MIS.*

MIS is not new. The private sector has been involved with the concept since the very beginning of electronic data processing. In contrast, the public sector appears to have taken a great deal of time to adopt the MIS concept. The scientific and management literature give the impression that it is mainly business and industry that are concerned with the management of information and with the design of information systems. This view is distorted, of course. Government is and always has been involved with managing information resources. Forest W. Horton and Donald A. Marchand (1982) refer to the United States Government's Paperwork Control Act of 1980, one of the consequences of which was the establishment of an Office of Federal Information Policy in the Office of Management and Budget. The role of the new office is to accomplish the five objectives of the act: (1) Reduce the information-processing burden by implementing uniform and consistent information policies and practices; (2) Increase the availability and accuracy of agency data and information; (3) Expand and strengthen federal information management activities; (4) Establish a single focal point for information management within the federal government, and (5) Decrease the paperwork burden on individuals, businesses, and state and local governments. Thus, although the road to more human information systems is difficult, one does on occasion come across very meaningful signs of encouragement.

My goal in writing this book is to introduce and to describe the new subject of the *human being* involved with all aspects of information systems, from the initial design stages to the management of such systems. This book addresses the administrator-manager-analyst-student-decision maker who wishes to obtain the sufficient and necessary knowledge which will enable him or her to consider numerous human factors in the design of organizational information systems. The orientation is straightforward: How to design an MIS which is (I hesitate to say it) more human. Is it possible? Have we solved enough technical problems related to MIS development that we may now look at certain *behavioral* aspects of such systems? For instance, during MIS design, how are we to consider and best utilize the decision makers' psychological and cognitive types?

There are two parts to *Managing Information Systems*:

**PART I** is the genesis of it all: an introduction to systems, information, systems analysis, and MIS. It is interesting to note that my first article on the subject of systems analysis dates back to 1970. The article, a popularization aimed at the manager, describes ". . . a recent discipline which does not yet have an underlying theory."

How times have changed! On the one hand, systems analysis has received numerous definitions, for there exist a great many books and articles dealing with its many facets. On the other hand, a theory is evolving which will render the discipline more teachable and more applicable. There is no doubt that the manager - be he or she of the private or public sector - is interested in systems analysis. Albeit, his or her preoccupations are oriented mainly toward certain types of systems such as management systems, data-processing systems and, of course, Management Information Systems (MIS). My goal in PART I of this book is to clarify the "system thing" and to furnish a sufficiently elaborate basis of knowledge about systems procedure to enable the reader to see the practical side of systems analysis. I wanted the presentation to be simple, direct, and concise. Nevertheless, PART I is not intended as a *vade mecum* on systems analysis. My ambition is the following: To render practical what is, at the offset, rather theoretical.

PART I is also an introduction to information systems and, more precisely, to MIS. This introduction is rather special, mainly because of two tests which the reader may find amusing and which will serve the purpose of establishing whether he or she can qualify as a member of the "Third Wave". If so, the reader may discover beforehand whether he or she has the necessary predisposition to consider the human within the system. I believe you will enjoy this part of the book.

**PART II** is the major portion of *Managing Information Systems*. It deals with the MIS design procedure. Whatever the reader's functions, tasks and responsibilities within an organization, he or she will discover that this part constitutes a practical guide to MIS design. It does not, however, ignore theoretical aspects and conceptual bases. These concepts are briefly reviewed and, in the predesign and design phases, eventually detail a global conceptual framework that constitutes a design for the organization's management information system which is more "human" than any of its predecessors. The central theme in this section can be summarized in one word: Humanization. The objective is clear: Establish a new design orientation, as well as the subsequent use of new design tools, which can be inserted within a human design framework.

If *Managing Information Systems* offers a promise of some kind, it just may be the following: an MIS designer, whether he or she is a manager or an analyst, informed and guided by this book's contents, will surely offer a most valid and valuable contribution to the improvement of his or her organization's information system. During the MIS design procedure, he or she will shed light on various and numerous organizational and informational elements. These elements will merge into a well-designed, well-implemented, and more human system, where better communications, more efficient processing and bureaucratic procedures assure not only an economy of time and money but also, and most importantly, a guarantee of improved decision-making by all members of the organization. All the rest - as it should - depends on the designer's ingenuity, competence, shrewdness, and artfulness.

The author sincerely thanks all of his colleagues and students who contributed both directly and indirectly to the research work and ensuing practical applications presented in this book.

I also wish to acknowledge the generous financial support of the School of Public Administration (École nationale d'administration publique (ÉNAP)) of the University of Québec which made it possible for most of the figures to be drawn and which offered the use of a word-processing system.

I would also like to express my sincere gratitude to Anne E. Johnson for her considerable help with the revisions.

Finally, the author is indebted (once again) to Suzanne Genois-Beaulieu for her extraordinary work in inputting the original manuscript in a word-processing system and, subsequently, for the numerous modifications prior to the *ouptut* of the final copy.

R. Hurtubise
Sillery, Québec, Canada
1 February, 1984.

PART I

# THE GENESIS OF IT ALL:
## Systems, Information, and Analysis

CHAPTER 1

# What Is a System?

Joël de Rosnay (1977, 1979), the best known French popularizer of systems analysis, suggested the following definition: "A system is a set of elements which interact dynamically and are organized to achieve a goal."

Yet there are as many versions of the definition of the word *system* as there are authors who have written on the subject. "A set of coordinated or structured parts", "the fulfillment of a mission, of a certain number of goals or objectives", and, "the accomplishment of one or many tasks" are but a few that have been put forward. The parts, or elements, of a system can also be numerous or few. The definitions tend to include social or abstract systems as well as physical or concrete systems. Thus, we speak of political, econometric, management, and information systems. We also refer to data-processing, telecommunication, and nervous systems. Even a sub-system is a system!

Unfortunately, what constitutes a system is still somewhat ambiguous. A look at the language of systems will start us on our way to systems theory and its application.

## THE KEY DEFINITIONS

To increase our understanding of what constitutes a system, I refer to T. H. Athey (1977), who presented definitions dealing with the composition of a system, its intent, and the relations between its own components and other systems. These definitions in a slightly modified form are:

**System composition**

| | |
|---|---|
| Component: | primary element composing the system |
| Link: | liaison (rapport, relation, interaction, reaction) between two components |

Boundary: localization of all components and links which can be directly influenced or controlled during the design of the system

Environment: encompasses all of the factors which influence the performance of the system but which remain uncontrollable

Interface: rendezvous shared by two systems, for example, where the outputs of one are the inputs of the other

## System intent

Globality: deals with the total aspects of a system and not with its individual components

Objective: desired result provided by the system

Mission: establishes itself via the relations of the system with its environment

Limit: the impossibility of a system responding equally well to all of its objectives

## System relationships

Hierarchy: the relations between systems or their components that are superior or subordinate to each other

Decision maker: principal client and future key user for whom the design is intended, an individual or a committee endowed with the authority to carry out changes by the system studies

Structure: the organization of the set of links and components of the system

Design: the appropriate choice of structure (components and their links) to attain the system objectives.

In using these definitions, it becomes possible to identify the properties, as well as the behavior, of the system under study. de Rosnay (1977, 116) has noted:

"The properties and the behavior of a complex system are determined by the internal organization and by its relations with its environment. To better understand these properties, to better predict this behaviour, is to utilize means which enable one to act on a system either by transforming it or by orienting its evolution."

There are three fundamental ideas related to system types: the closed system, the open system, and feedback.

The *closed system* is *closed* to its environment; only the links, liaisons, interactions and reactions that are internal to it exist. There is no transfer of anything — data, information, matter, energy — to or from the environment.

The *open system* is *open* to its environment; the relations are maintained and data, information, matter and energy are exchanged with the environment.

*Feedback* is a *loop* linking an output back to an input. What a system produces can influence what it needs in order to produce. The feedback loop incorporates a very important contribution to cybernetics, the science of command processes in machines and in robots.[1] Negative feedback — the compensating or regulating kind — seeks a stable state (homeostasis) by converging toward a goal after 'leaving' an initial departure state. The thermostat of a home heating system is an example. Positive feedback, on the other hand, tends toward an unstable state by increasing the divergence from the initial departure state. Alvin Toffler (1980) cites rather striking examples: The heating system or the thermostat which, instead of putting out the flame, ignites it; the game of Monopoly in which the more money a player has, the more property can be bought, the more rents will be received, and the more that player will again buy; and finally, the arms race between the East and the West.

These three ideas (open system, closed system, and feedback) are peculiar to the systems approach. They are relatively new. Before a system idea was created, another approach had long been the mode: the classical, scientific method of analysis.

# FROM SCIENTIFIC METHOD TO SYSTEMS THEORY

The scientific method places the phenomenon to be studied into a controlled environment and systematically examines all of the variables implied by the research hypotheses. Even though this approach has brought about a certain understanding of the world around us, many researchers were and are impeded by its inherent limitations. The genesis of systems theory is attributed to a biologist who was so impeded.

L. von Bertalanffy (1968) found the scientific method inadequate to explain certain complex biological phenomena. He felt that everything is a system and that systems possess properties which are common regardless of the disciplines in which they evolve. His *systems theory* proposed to explain the functioning of systems by considering the links or relations between the simple elements which compose systems.[2] In developing such systems concepts as globality, relations, environment, and mission (the foundations of his theory), Bertalanffy created tools that researchers have used since his time and in all fields of human endeavor. Scientists, business professionals and others have discovered the power of systems theory as a way to study phenomena by situating them *in* their environment and by considering their global behavior before examining that of their components. The systems approach is global, macroscopic.[3]

If a systems theory does exist, a systems logic — an approach —must also, and the accompanying principles of that logic should apply to different sectors and to all disciplines. The idea is not new. Pascal wrote in 1650 or thereabouts:

"The parts of the world all have such a relation and a connection to one another that I believe it is impossible to know one without the other and without the whole." (Lasfargues 1976, 36).

This global approach is especially powerful in permitting a consciousness of complex and complicated systems. More specifically, it permits an awareness of the links and liaisons between components. It situates each component with respect to the whole (the global system) and illuminates the system's functioning by appreciating beforehand all interactions between components. The systems approach, while not at all suggesting there is no longer a need to study individual components, advocates: Don't miss the forest for the trees!

The two fundamental principles of the systems approach are (1) a total or global perspective of the phenomena which make up the system, and (2) an emphasis on the study of all the links between system components. The application of the approach is, appropriately enough, systems analysis! Practically speaking, it is an analysis-synthesis-design procedure. A definition of these four concepts plus one important addition will help clarify this.

1. *Analysis* suggests a decomposition, a dissociation of a whole into its constituent parts

2. *Synthesis* on the other hand, suggests proceeding from a simple to the composite, from component elements to a whole

3.  A *design* is a creative plan resulting from an intellectual activity, from acts of human intelligence

4.  A *procedure* is a way, the systematic steps, the tools used, to achieve a certain result

5.  Finally, a *problem* suggests a question, a difficulty that warrants solving, a need that warrants filling

## TWO WORDS OF CAUTION

In closing this chapter, two words of caution are necessary. First, even though systems analysis is based on the systems approach, numerous analysts find it difficult to distinguish between the *systems* approach and the *systematic* approach. The latter consists simply in addressing a problem systematically by undertaking a series of actions sequentially in a detailed fashion. Nothing is left to chance, and nothing is forgotten. This is the most frequent type of analysis. It is based on the classical scientific approach, the Cartesian. Our second word of caution requires a brief description of the Cartesian method, described in 1637 by René Descartes (Lasfargues 1976, 18-19) in his famous *Discourse on the Method:*

". . . instead of the great number of precepts of which logic is composed, I believed that the *four* following would suffice, providing that I take a firm and constant resolution never to miss observing them. The *first* was never to consider anything as being true unless I knew it to be obviously so; the *second*, to divide each of the difficulties that I examined in as many parcels as possible . . . to better solve them. The *third*, to conduct my thoughts by order, starting with the simplest . . . so as to build little by little, . . . until knowledge is gained on the more composite, and by assuming order between those which do not naturally precede one another. And the *last*, to undertake everywhere enumerations so complete and revisions so general that I was assured not to have forgotten anything."

The *Cartesian method* is a logic based on a deduction which proceeds from the simple to the complex. In systems terms, the application or the procedure related to this method may be enumerated as:

1.  Delimit and define the system which must be analyzed

2. Divide the system into components sufficiently simple that they can be analyzed

3. Analyze each component

4. Assemble the components to restore the given system

This method is powerful only when the system is simple. It is difficult to apply when the system is the least bit complex! Let us consider, for example, the second phase. How is one to go about dividing the system into its components? Descartes did not define any subdivision rules. As a matter of fact, to this day, no one has!

The moral? It is difficult to assemble simple elements when the global phenomenon is neither an addition nor a juxtaposition of constituent elements. The Cartesian method is fine for those situations in which the behavior of the simple elements of a system is unchanged by the forces of interaction with other elements. Yet it does not consider interactions! It does not take into account the links between system components! What then is the method, the logic, the tools for understanding complex, interacting systems?

# CHAPTER 2

# The Systems Method: Procedure and Tools

*Systems analysis* is a discipline. Nevertheless, the ambition in Part I of this book is not so much to present a formal definition of the discipline nor to elaborate a general theory which would apply to every field, rather, it is to clarify what systems analysis is —its method and procedural tools.

Systems analysis does not only pursue academic knowledge and the elaboration of a methodology. Its ultimate aim is to influence events in the real world. This art/science (you choose) seeks to optimize the decision-making process in a context of change, complexity, and uncertainty by studying objectives and options which will, in turn, permit the attainment of the objectives. Such a study can only be accomplished by a systems procedure which utilizes tools that are qualitative as well as quantitative in nature.

The distinguishing feature of systems analysis is its method, a procedure that differs significantly from the Cartesian. M. Landry and J.-L. Malouin (1976), and Joël de Rosnay (1975) have developed excellent comparisons of the two methods (tables 1, p.10 and 2, p. 11). It would be erroneous, however, to suggest that these two procedures are incompatible; they are quite complementary! Yet during a systems analysis, the Cartesian is a subordinate procedure. The set of steps and the tools of the systems method are unique to a global view.

## THE SYSTEMS PROCEDURE IN FIVE STEPS

The systems procedure is comprised of five steps. One must (1) define the problem, (2) establish and weight success criteria, (3) generate solutions, (4) evaluate solutions, and (5) select an optimal system.

TABLE 1

## COMPARISON OF THE SCIENTIFIC METHOD AND THE SYSTEMS APPROACH TO COMPLEX PHENOMENA

| | Objective pursued: | Abstract model developed by: | Knowledge to be acquired: | Observation point at outset: |
|---|---|---|---|---|
| SCIENTIFIC METHOD | Global knowledge | Additivity of knowledge pertaining to simple elements | Explanation, reproduction, and prediction; normative | Elements and their characteristics |
| SYSTEMS APPROACH | Global knowledge | Decomposition of an observed global phenomenon | Description, and prediction | Global behavior of phenomenon and system structure |

From: (Landry, M., Malouin, J.-L., La complémentarité des approches systémique et scientifique dans le domaine des sciences humaines (Complementarity of the Systems and Scientific Approaches in the Human Sciences), *Relations Industrielles*, vol. 31, no. 3, 1976. Les Presses de L'Université Laval, Québec. (By permission.)

## TABLE 2

## COMPARISON OF THE ANALYTICAL APPROACH
## AND THE SYSTEMS APPROACH

| ANALYTICAL APPROACH | SYSTEMS APPROACH |
| --- | --- |
| Isolates: Centers on the elements | Links: Centers on the interaction between the elements |
| Considers the nature of the interactions | Considers the effects of the interactions |
| Based on precision of details | Based on the global view |
| Modifies one variable at a time | Modifies groups of variables simultaneously |
| Time independent: The phenomena studied are considered reversible | Integrates time and irreversibility |
| Facts validated by experimental proof associated with a theory | Facts validated by comparing model with reality |
| Precise detailed models which are difficult to implement (e.g., econometrics models) | Models not sufficiently rigorous to acquire knowledge, but can be used for decision and action (e.g., Club of Rome models) |
| Efficient approach when the interactions are linear and weak | Efficient approach when the interactions are nonlinear and strong |
| Leads to unidisciplinary teaching | Leads to multidisciplinary teaching |
| Leads to detailed programmed action | Leads to objective-oriented action |
| Knowledge of details, goals are ill-defined | Knowledge of goals, details are imprecise |

(de Rosnay, J., *Le macroscope, vers une vision globale*, (The Macroscope, Towards a Global View), Editions du Seuil, Paris, 1975, page 110. By permission.)

*Problem definition or need formulation.*

This step describes the given phenomenon in terms of one or more problems to be resolved, challenges to be met, objectives to be attained, and systems to be corrected, optimized and designed. This phase is essentially one of reconnaissance and identification, enunciation and classification, critique, and evaluation of the problem. The definition and formulation step specifies the performance measures, the resources involved, and the associated environment.

Three important points warrant examination during the problem definition phase. They are the notions of *problem*, of *objectivity*, and of *who* defines the problem or formulates the need.

First a *problem* exists when an individual perceives a gap between an existing and a desired state and decides to intervene. If the word *problem* is problematic, you may substitute *challenge* or *need*.

Second, *objectivity* is a quality, it is free of partialities and prejudices and thus gives a more faithful representation than the subjective point-of-view. Yet the real world as perceived by an observer is greatly influenced by an observation post and by subjective values. In systems analysis, objectivity must become a state of mind, because the analyst will have to examine and judge in as impartial a manner as possible.

Closely linked to the notion of objectivity is a question: Who defines the problem? The very behavior, nature, and position of the problem definer influence the definition, scope, and complexity of the problem.

The definer must not only discover the needs (which are almost always ill-defined), but must also translate them in terms of specific problems that can be studied. This task requires an ability to separate the important from the unimportant, the pertinent from the superficial. In general, an individual who is knowledgeable of analysis methods or procedural techniques has an advantage because (theoretically) this person can establish the essence of a problem even in fields which are new to him or her.

*Establishment and weighting of success criteria.*

This step requires listing the principles which will be used to judge the system options or solutions. The major quantitative task is to assign a weighting factor to each criterion noted. Weighting factors are expressed in terms of relative weights; that is, it has a significance only when expressed and compared with another criterion's factor. For example, a criterion of weighting factor 5 is five times more important than a criterion of weighting factor 1, but only half as important as the criterion of weighting factor 10. These relative weights determine the importance and equilibrium that must accompany the analyst's judgement during the evaluation of system options (the next phase). The effort is straightforward: Put variables in concrete form and quantify them — even those which may appear at first glance to be qualitative in nature, but which may serve to evaluate and eventually to select and retain an option. Once again, maximum objectivity is essential. As well, it is very important that the list of success criteria be established before any attempt be made to generate the options.

*Generation of system options or solutions.*

During this step the analyst really studies the system and realizes that complex phenomena cannot be understood by simply dividing them into their composite parts. Rather, it is a global view of the entire given system that enables the analyst to explain its functioning. This is the systems frame of mind. In effect, when one is confronted with a set of interdependent elements - such as individuals sharing responsibilities, physical elements mutually interacting, activities closely linked together, one cannot "divide each of the difficulties in as many parcels as possible". A global view is required. From this view will flow the options.

*Evaluation of system options or solutions.*

This step links the success criteria with the system options. The link is a substudy that evaluates, in as quantative a fashion as possible, each option generated in accordance with the set of weighted criteria (figure 1, p. 14). In its simplest form, the task consists in assigning, for each criterion, a value for each option. The values assigned indicate to what extent the options satisfy a criteria. This evaluation is carried out line by line, criterion by criterion. Once all of the values are established, two simple mathematical operations ensue: Multiply each value in a given line by its corresponding weighting factor and, for each option column, add the resulting products and obtain a total which is the sum of the weighted values for each option. For example, a value 10 assigned to an option indicates that it fully meets the criterion. On the other hand, a value 5 assigned to another option could indicate that, firstly, it only partially meets (at the 50% level) the requirement imposed by the given criterion and, secondly, its performance related to the given

## FIGURE 1

## EVALUATION OF SYSTEM OPTIONS
## AS A FUNCTION OF SUCCESS CRITERIA

| LIST OF CRITERIA | | SYSTEM OPTIONS | | | | |
|---|---|---|---|---|---|---|
| | weighting factors: | OPTION 1 | OPTION 2 | OPTION 3 | | OPTION N |
| CRITERION 1 | $P_1$ | value: $V_{11}$ | $V_{12}$ | $V_{13}$ | ┆ | $V_{1N}$ |
| CRITERION 2 | $P_2$ | $V_{21}$ | $V_{22}$ | $V_{23}$ | ┆ | $V_{2N}$ |
| CRITERION 3 | $P_3$ | $V_{31}$ | $V_{32}$ | $V_{33}$ | ┆ | $V_{3N}$ |
| | | | | | ┆ | |
| CRITERION M | $P_M$ | $V_{M1}$ | $V_{M2}$ | $V_{M3}$ | ┆ | $V_{MN}$ |
| WEIGHTED SUM OF OPTIONS | | $P_1 \times V_{11}$ $+$ $P_2 \times V_{21}$ $+$ $P_3 \times V_{31}$ $+$ $\vdots$ $+$ $P_M \times V_{M1}$ | $P_1 \times V_{12}$ $+$ $P_2 \times V_{22}$ $+$ $P_3 \times V_{32}$ $+$ $\vdots$ $+$ $P_M \times V_{M2}$ | $P_1 \times V_{13}$ $+$ $P_2 \times V_{23}$ $+$ $P_3 \times V_{33}$ $+$ $\vdots$ $+$ $P_M \times V_{M3}$ | | $P_1 \times V_{1N}$ $+$ $P_2 \times V_{2N}$ $+$ $P_3 \times V_{3N}$ $+$ $\vdots$ $+$ $P_M \times V_{MN}$ |

criterion is but half that noted for the first option.

It is in this manner that a quantitative and relative evaluation of the various system options can be obtained. Such an evaluation — even if it is approximate — can be extremely useful to the systems analyst, who now has a quantitative and more objective estimate of what could have remained merely a very qualitative and subjective feeling.

*The selection and retention of the optimal system.*

Theoretically, the option which obtains the highest score is the one selected. The substudy should bring together all considerations, both criteria and options, which illuminate the best or optimal solution. Yet, everything is relative! Thus, *best* or *optimal* are exclusive within the confines and the territory of the particular analysis.

In ending this description of the five-step systems procedure, one cannot help but reflect on another procedure, that of the human decision-making process. Herbert A. Simon (1977) exposed what is, in effect, a framework for information systems design. The conceptual framework described is decision oriented, is based on behavioral sciences, and describes the decision-making process in four phases: (1) intelligence (knowledge) about the environment and the identification of conditions that require action, (2) design (establishment) of options as a result of the preceding step, (3) choice (selection) of a particular action among the options enumerated during the previous step, and (4) review or evaluation of past choices. Compare Simon's four phases with the five steps of the systems procedure. How elegant the match of the systems procedure with that of human behavior in the decision-making process!

## An Application: The Feasibility Study

A feasibility study is often the first opportunity an analyst or manager has to undertake a systems analysis. Because this type of study is of rather short duration (a few days or weeks), it offers an interesting opportunity to apply the systems procedure.

Generally, the objective of a feasibility study is to justify a system of some kind by determining its return on investment, its ease of implementation, its deficiencies or lack of other options and its effects on other important factors. The formal proposal leading to such a study or project must include objectives and procedures to be used, dates, costs, and any other information deemed necessary. On the other hand, the final report will contain (1) the problem definition,

(2) the constraints and boundaries of the system under study, (3) the desired results, (4) the system options (problem solutions), (5) the design concept, (6) a cost-benefit analysis, (7) the development phases, (8) implementation dates, (9) cost considerations, (10) personnel requirements (including expertise and training), (11) the risks involved, (12) the chances of success, user involvement and, finally, (13) the recommendations.[4]

Five principal consequences resulting from a feasibility study include: (1) a basis for establishing priorities and allocating resources, (2) a demonstration that the project is compatible with organizational goals and objectives, (3) a familiarization (mainly by management) with the methods which can be used, the chances of success, and the risks involved, (4) one or more system options or solutions, and (5) a demonstration or a proof that the organization's systems division can design and develop the given system.

## TOOLS OF THE TRADE

The systems procedure uses powerful tools. In this section, I will describe several in some detail and refer the avid reader to additional sources on all. I will speak of models; list both quantitative and qualitative techniques, including explanations of two (The Delphi and Brainstorming) that are exceptionally well suited to systems analysis; and emphasize the advantages of the multidisciplinary team approach.

## MODELS

In my description of a system I have not distinguished between the real system and the picture or representation the analyst creates. The analyst does indeed use a model, a smaller representation of the original. That is, the analyst works by analogy.

The particular methodology of systems analysis depends upon building and using different models at different stages in the systems procedure. The goal is to gain knowledge of the problem at hand — to test, simulate, design, or manipulate in ways impossible in the real world.[5] Furthermore, the use of models can assure communication and cooperation among analysts, managers, decision makers, and others who may intervene during the study.

Models can classify systems, analyze variables and their influences and, finally, represent various system options.

J.L. LeMoigne (1977, 216) describes "how to go about using systems theory in practice." He coins the word *systemography* and illustrates uses for design, analysis, and simulation of system models according to five key parameters: missions, environment, structure, functions and evolvement (Figure 2). Systemography is applied to the three types of models as follows:

"1.  For a *design*, one would identify the missions (1) in an environment (2) and then afterwards imagine a structure (3) which finally would be made to function (4) and evolve (5) in accordance with the missions in the environment.

2.  For an *analysis*, one would start off with the functions (1) or with the evolvement (2) which we observe in an environment (3); we would interpret them according to some missions (4) and would then infer a structure (5) which can assume them.

## FIGURE 2

## SYSTEMOGRAPHY:
## SEQUENCE OF PARAMETERS FOR
## THREE SYSTEMS MODELS

MISSIONS ENVIRONMENT STRUCTURE FUNCTIONS EVOLVEMENTS

DESIGN

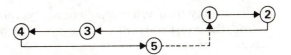

ANALYSIS
(SYSTEMS)

SIMULATION

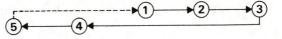

3. For a *simulation*, one would start off with a structure (1), previously obtained by design or analysis; one would make it function (2) and evolve (3) in an environment (4) and one would compare the results of this activity with the contemplated missions (5)."

Thus it is seen that the analyst must create a model of the system to be studied that is as faithful a representation as possible of that system. Yet, model building is but one tool. Others have been developed and successfully applied.

## Quantitative Techniques

Many systems analysis tools issued from a discipline which was at the height of its popularity in the 1950s: Operations research. OR was responsible for quantitative techniques based on quite sophisticated mathematics. Herbert A. Simon (1977, 57) has listed these mathematical tools as well as examples of fields where these tools can aid management decision making.

1. Linear programming for the operations of a gasoline refinery and for commercial cattle-feed manufacturing

2. Dynamic programming for inventory and production planning

3. Integer programming for planning and scheduling problems that must have discrete rather than continuous solutions

4. Game theory to represent marketing problems

5. Queuing theory to handle scheduling tasks and other problems involving waiting lines

6. Bayesian decision theory for making choices among alternatives under uncertainty about outcomes

7. Probability theory, a component of several of the other tools, and the most versatile, has been used directly in a wide variety of contexts.

## Qualitative Techniques

In addition to the quantitative tools listed above, a growing number of managers have used graphical representation techniques such as Program Evaluation and Review Technique (PERT) and the

Critical Path Method (CPM) for project management purposes (Moder and Philips, 1970). Case studies and simulation games are modeling tools, also, and are not based exclusively on mathematics. Two very important and useful tools of relatively recent development fit nicely into systems analysis. They are the Delphi method and Brainstorming.

These are also nonmathematical procedural tools. Both are described below because they illustrate exceptionally well the central theme of systems analysis — the *links* between the component parts of the system.

DELPHI: Consensus on the Future

Since its development by Dalkey and Helmer (1963) at the Rand Corporation, the Delphi method has been applied thousands of times in a variety of fields.[6] Delphi is a consultive procedure where participants usually experts in a particular field, are asked to explain their ideas about the future of a variable or a system. It is unnecessary for the future to be very far off.

Although a consultive procedure, it does not require face-to-face meetings between participants. It does involve, however, an iteration between them and the organizers.

Each participant receives an initial structured questionnaire which includes instructions and a description of the Delphi's objectives. The questionnaire consists of a set of elements using similar or different scales which may be qualitative or quantitative in nature. Answers to questions generated by organizers or by respondents should be numerical so that they may be summarized in terms of statistical distributions (mean, median, deviation).

The iteration of questions and answers is pursued between the organizers and the participants until the answers converge. In general, this procedure lasts four or five rounds or a few weeks. During this dialogue, the organizers situate each participant's answer within the set of answers and informs each of his or her opinion with respect to the statistical median. If the answer falls within the first or fourth quartile, the participant knows that his or her response is deviant. The participant can then revise or maintain the answer. So may the respondent whose answer is close to the median. In most Delphis, the iteration procedure results in the convergence of answers. One very important point: individual responses are kept confidential.

BRAINSTORMING: The Design Ideas

Brainstorming is one of the best known group free-association techniques. Developed by Alex Osborn (1952), it has been successfully used in many fields.

The number of participants in a brainstorming session should be less than twenty; six to twelve persons should suffice. Superiors and subordinates should not participate together. Nor should participants have the same jobs or the same education. The technique works best if some participants have little knowledge of the problem at hand. One or two experts may be employed as a source of information, but their very presence may hinder the spontaneity of the other participants either because of "professional shyness" or because of the opinions these experts may express.

The problem studied and the level of discussion should be clearly specified before the brainstorming session. One, and only one, problem should be studied. The problem should not be all-embracing, otherwise the solutions put forth will be superficial or even suggest subproblems to be solved. If the problem's scope is too wide, subproblems will have to be defined and addressed before proceeding any further. At the beginning of a brainstorming session, the chairperson informs the participants of the rules which will be enforced. Osborn has proposed four rules:[7]

1. All forms of criticism are forbidden! All opinions or judgements related to the solutions or ideas expressed should be kept until a later evaluation phase.

2. Total freedom of thought and liberty of expression are preferred. The more extravagant the ideas, the better! It is easier to destroy an extravagant idea than to create one.

3. Quantity is important! The more ideas and solutions there are, the better are the chances of generating good ones.

4. The combination, association and optimization of ideas is called for. In addition to forwarding personal ideas, the participants should propose improvements to others' ideas and combine two or three ideas to create a better solution.

Four other rules aimed at increasing the participants' efficiency during a brainstorming session are:

1. Questions judged impertinent will not be answered. They should be asked beforehand. Questions imply a form of

evaluation of ideas and may destroy the creative tempo. For this reason extraneous discussion is also prohibited.

2. The participants should not discuss or defend their ideas. Ideas should be expressed concisely and precisely, and quickly.

3. What is obvious should not be rejected or neglected; omitting the obvious is rendering a judgement, and repeating an idea brings about a different and better way of expressing and interpreting it.

4. When things slow down, the chairperson should read the third or fifth idea to stimulate thought.

A brainstorming session is not, and should not be, a group decision-making effort. The session is held to stimulate the design of ideas, which is just a part of the decision-making process. A brainstorming session has one goal: the generation of a great number of ideas by the free association resulting from interactions between participants. Evaluation is not forgotten, but should take place later during the systems or solutions evaluation phase. If the objectives of a session are well defined, if the participants are free to express themselves, and if the session rules are respected, the session is likely to generate many ideas, powerful strategies, optimal solutions, and elegant systems.

## The Multidisciplinary Team

Systems analysis is not a "black box" into which problems are cast and from which solutions are ejected! Systems analysis is above and beyond anything else a highly creative process, a function of the human resources — *human* — involved in the analysis. The solutions and designs resulting from the study effort are not necessarily explicit from the data and objectives of the given system. More often than not, conceptual frameworks are incomplete and somewhat ambiguous. Imagination, judgment, and courage are required, if for no other reason than the fact that the set of future environments and the proposed system options will have to be imagined and classified, and their possible consequences evaluated. For these reasons, a multidisciplinary team approach is most effective for complex systems studies.[8] Such a team calls on the imaginative skills of both specialists and generalists. And, although the members of the team possess various abilities and varied training, their dominating quality must be an ability to communicate with each other and with the analyst.

The team will be guided and coordinated by the systems analyst.

This person may start with a basic knowledge. Yet because systems analysis is a relatively recent discipline, because the theoretical basis is still under development, and because much of it is still at the philosophical stage, the analyst will develop additional abilities as the particular systems study progresses.

As a discipline and as a management tool, systems analysis offers numerous opportunities for multidisciplinary team work, a team effort that can effect a most useful synthesis and adaptation of techniques belonging to the various professions. The requisite attitude may seem brutal: We are all ignorant! What may help is that each one of us ignores different things! It is this attitude which enables each multidisciplinary team member's inputs to be processed and transformed into collective outputs from which better performing system designs ensue.

The design I am approaching is that for a Management Information System. A multidisciplinary team is particularly apropos for an MIS design effort. An MIS creates, coordinates, and allows control of information. Therefore, before we expose the specific tasks of the multidisciplinary team, we must look at information — at what it is and what it is not. We will look also at data processing as merely a component of an organization's information needs, and at several crucial attitudes and errors of top management.

# CHAPTER 3

# What Is Information?

The dictionary certainly does not help very much! Information theory helps to refine our understanding of it, but is mostly concerned with message variety.[9] Information as related to cybernetics addresses neither content nor signification; it does not concern what we are saying, but rather what we could say. Nor is information synonymous with data.

Rather, information is the signification that we give to data; information is related to the context in which data and information are received, and to the person who receives. A piece of data that tells us what we already know is not information! Richard Leifer of Rensselaer Polytechnic Institute has offered the best definition I have seen: "Information is an input which reduces uncertainty, whereas data constitute an input which does not."[10] Information is also both power and energy.

Information is power. Indeed, information has been used, is used and will definitely be used, to help play - and win - organizational games! An individual who controls information within an organization is very powerful. This person can create or reduce artificial uncertainties and bias, and can manipulate people and events by retaining or communicating certain information. There is a danger, however. By manipulating information destined for others within an organization, the transmitted information loses its original significance and may adversely affect the receiver and the organization.

Information is also energy. Energy must be spent to obtain information. Conversely, information is required to obtain energy. Another notion related to energy and information is *entropy*. Entropy is the opposite of information. Where a system "loses" information, there is an increase in entropy.

An excellent definition of information comes from LeMoigne (1978): "Information is a formatted object (endowed with identifiable forms) *artificially created* by the human being to represent a type of event which he can perceive and identify in the real world." (Emphasis added.) This definition is superb! It helps establish our point of view with regard to what information should be: Information is what the decision maker needs in order to decide!

# INFORMATION, DATA PROCESSING, AND SYSTEMS

"Information system" does not necessarily imply "computer". In fact, a systems analysis of an organization might very well demonstrate that the solution to management information needs is not a computer with all its software and specialized personnel, but rather a well-managed filing cabinet! However, the computer and, more specifically, electronic data-processing (EDP) certainly acts as a catalyst to reconsidering and rationalizing the organization's existing information system. The points of view furnished by applying the systems approach provides the manager with a clear distinction between data, data-processing, and information. It also forces the data-processing specialist to be less of a computer analyst and more of an information analyst!

# A SYSTEMS APPROACH TO EDP

Today, the use of systems analysis to design data-processing systems is a foregone conclusion. This was not always the case!

In the old days, knowing little or nothing of computers, the user attempted to define the information needs of an organization. The computer specialist ridiculed the user's attempts, considered the defined needs highly exagerated, and rewrote the project specifications. At this point, an analyst analyzed and rewrote yet another project, after which a programmer modified the analyst's version and wrote a program. Everyone was unhappy. Each blamed the other. Some blamed even the computer! Note the lack of coordination in this way of proceeding. Note, too, the lack of awareness of the links.

In a data-processing project, as in a management information system, everything is connected, and information and data-processing needs evolve.

Data-processing is only one of the many interdependent elements linked to the organization's mission, goals, and objectives. During the design of a data-processing system tayloristic work-division principles do not apply! Only a systems team under the supervision of an informed management can take into account the various interactions in the organization and their perpetually evolving needs. Therefore, it is essential that subteams be associated with each project and that the systems team coordinate all of the organization's data-processing projects.

Part II of this book will address the MIS challenge. As we near the conclusion of this first part, one final and short example may illustrate how systems analysis principles can be applied to the organization's information needs.

Systems language is somewhat abstract. Yet it can be rendered in terms of the organization's information system. *Input, processing, output,* and *feedback* are the systems terms. In the organization, these translate to *information, decision, action,* and *control.* Once a decision-making situation has been identified and described, the manager gathers information, determines what must be done, and chooses the best solution. The choice is executed and then controlled by a follow up. An organizational loop is established. The follow up is fed back into the decision-making process.

## TOP MANAGEMENT SHOULD KNOW . . .

In addressing the subjects of information, data-processing, and systems, we must emphasize the importance of top management. No project, no system, will be successful if management is not well informed and supportive. Yet, embarrassingly often, organizational information strategies fail. The single prerequisite for effective systems design, for which top management must take responsibility, is the presence of the basic elements that enable an objective analysis. If the logical standards that apply to all fields are not respected, the usefulness of an analysis can be compromised, not because of the analytical tools, but because of the tools' users. Thus, top management must have sufficient knowledge of, and be more sympathetic toward, the objectives and the methods of systems analysis. Such a comprehension sensed at all levels of management increases dramatically the chances of success.

Why are there difficulties with information systems? What happens? How is it that an organization which can clearly identify its objectives and minutely plan its activities can, under the heading *Systems Analysis,* develop an information strategy so ill adapted to its real needs?

A great number of difficulties arise from *attacking* the challenge at the conceptual level with a complex team of many analysts. Severe management, motivational, and communication problems can arise within a team, especially if management requires that the team choose among various equipment concepts such as micro-and minicomputers, computer networks, distributed processing, and data bases.

In addition to cumbersome team size, management, at the beginning of a study, too often assigns the best analysts to management positions. The effect is immediate. Top analysts cannot work directly or exclusively on the problem at hand. Rather, they become involved with the organization's paper battles and with the creation of mini-empires.

Motivational problems also are associated with a team made up of numerous persons. Often an analyst responsible for specific tasks becomes withdrawn from the organization's merit system to the point that his or her own goal becomes that of minimizing risks in order that the subsystem analysis be accepted. Superfluous and conservative designs are the direct result.

A postulate may now be stated: The number and dimension of practical problems which an information strategy study will confront are directly proportional to the number of analysts making up the systems team. When a decision is complex but extremely important, only a small number of persons should be assigned to the task. Because most errors relate to team membership, size, and structure, top management must

- use talented analysts,
- have fewer people in the analysis team,
- spend less money, and more time on the study,
- demand fewer details from the analysts, and
- distinguish between a concepts or strategy study and a detailed preliminary design.

Top management's fundamental error related to data-processing and information strategy is precisely the difference between data-processing and information. Data processing is but a tool, whereas information - more precisely, management information - is what binds the organization together.

# CHAPTER 4

# How Is The MIS Different?

I have suggested a new definition of the word *information:* information is what the decision maker needs to make a decision. In the context of an organization, information is an important resource that clearly warrants managing. Yet can it be managed? Furthermore, what changes will management need to make in its information sector, and why?

## BUILDING TOWARD BETTER DECISIONS

Every organization has one or more information systems for its various levels. These systems have always existed. Their goal consists in retrieving daily operational data, which can then be processed and used to prepare reports that correspond to management needs. Managers of all levels must make frequent choices, selecting from a number of possibilities, not only to attain organizational objectives but also to operate, control, plan, and supervise (Simon 1977). Decision making is the motor of the organization, the culmination of all managerial effort.

Traditionally, the approach to controlling information has been to drown management under an unremitting flow of paper. In recent years, managers and analysts have realized that a more efficacious approach supplies each decision maker with information specific to each decision-making situation.[11] This realization suggests that an evolutionary system should be designed so that specific data will be transformed into information for operational and control purposes and be further refined to serve top management planning purposes.

The Management Information System, the MIS, is the evolutionary design! With it, the various organizational units use one system, a system that exploits computer technology and makes full use of data, information, and human resources. In converting data into information and information into significant actions, an MIS provides tools for all levels of management so that subsystems function adequately. The MIS facilitates decision-making processes at all levels of the organization (Eldin and Croft 1974)

The MIS is modeled on the organization's structure and is built by progressively integrating data, programs, software, hardware, operational and administrative procedures, and personnel into a well-structured set that accounts for the organizational functions.[12] The MIS is designed to assist its users—that is, all members of the organization. Therefore, it can include a great number of individual but integrated subsystems of three basic types: *operational systems* that process data belonging to basic operations (inventory, wages, turn-around time, etc.); *reporting systems* that inform the various organizational levels (often the same information in varying formats to increase reporting efficiency, quality, and pertinence at each level); and *decision support systems* for both recurrent and one-time situations (Stanford Research Institute 1970).

Again, the mission is decision. To this end, an effective MIS will be selective and pertinent. It will discriminate between and create the three basic subsystems in an integrated way so that all elements are considered in relation to each other and so that the decisional effects can be easily measured. The MIS is flexible; it represents a synthesis of each manager's changing information needs and takes into account his or her decision-making responsibilities. Viewed from its most elementary state, the MIS is a process which transforms data into information. Viewed from its most evolved state, it is a process that allows informed decision.

# EACH PERSON CONTRIBUTES

An MIS enables managers to be better informed about the functioning of the various operational units, systems, and subsystems of the organization. This new approach is thus very useful if for no other reason than that it coordinates the organization into an information network. Although the method is relatively new to most practicing managers, they are very well aware that management is in full development, in full evolution. They know also the importance of good decision making, and that timely and accurate information is crucial to that process.

Consequently, the first step to the development of an MIS is to establish information needs. Top management in conjunction with division managers must rigorously define their needs. They are the only ones who understand both their milieu and their resources. Unfortunately, they are generally not MIS specialists. Their ability to study and to define information needs is usually constrained by daily operational considerations. The help of an MIS analyst is needed. But not just any analyst. Rapport between the analyst and management is extremely important. These key people must share a similar global view in order to carry out the design procedure in such a way that the organization's information responds and corresponds to the social reality of the organization.

Furthermore, although top management will be served by the information system, it must eventually respond to all user needs. Thus the MIS cannot be modeled on one user or group. Each and every member of the organization will become a user. Each has a contribution to make toward its design and development. Top management's role is central. It gives the impetus for the effort. In its determination to see the effort through to completion and in its utilizing of the creativity and knowledge of all potential users, top management creates an organization-wide atmosphere of confidence that allows the successful implementation of the new system.

## A COMMUNICATION'S PERSPECTIVE

If each organization has an information system, it also has a network structured to communicate information. Unfortunately, "information" and "communication" are so often used interchangeably that it is somewhat difficult to use one without implying the other. Communication's theory has much to offer (Longpré 1980). Here, I will briefly review a few concepts in order to clarify the distinction and relate one to the other.

For there to be communication, at least two parties are required: an emitter encodes a message and a receiver decodes it. The receiver does not perceive the message in its entirety, but rather registers what is pertinent and assigns a meaning to it according to his or her frames of reference. In fact, when a message is transmitted from one subject to another, a semantic approximation is always implied. The message content, full of its meaning, becomes information. Thus, meaning is the link between communication and information.

In an organization, a primary function of the communication's network consists in coherently linking each member in a synergy that attains objectives. We have seen previously that an MIS involves inputs, processing, outputs, and a feedback loop. Communication's theory amplifies this schema with the encoding and decoding phenomena and relates them to the information-decision continuum (figure 3, p. 31).

A basic means of communicating the information needed to reach a decision is the report. The actions ensuing, however, will be appropriate only if the reports are accurate, pertinent, timely, and clear. Periodic evaluation of reports is a management must.

# EVALUATING MANAGEMENT REPORTS

A reporting system is an integral part of an organization's communications network. These ad hoc systems are generally designed and installed in a very intuitive if not unconscious fashion. Yet, although they do function and are used, more and more managers wish to improve their existing system. Because the MIS concept is being taught at all levels and through business conferences, management is receiving the message of change and is learning of the new approach.

Initially, management must critically evaluate current reports (Hurtubise 1981). What information do they really contain? Are they reliable? To the point? Timely? Each person who receives or generates a report is in a unique position to answer these questions. Figure 4 (p. 32) is an evaluation form which can be filled out by each person in the current reporting system (Gallagher 1974). One evaluation form is filled out per report. The appraiser may remain anonymous or may identify her-or himself. The title of the report is then noted. Appraisers evaluate in two ways: by associating a cost to the report and by expressing opinions according to a scale for each of twenty-six opposing adjective pairs. In this way subjective opinions are quantified.

Such evaluations will surely be useful to management because they attract attention to both the problem areas and the well-functioning areas of the existing information-reporting system. The resulting consciousness may even bring about a desire to design a Management Information System. The use of the report form is the first step toward more fully utilizing an organization's personnel, the human within the system.

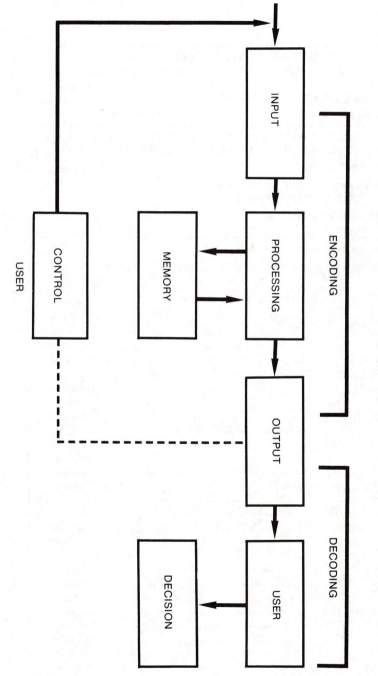

FIGURE 3

A MIS AS VIEWED FROM
THE COMMUNICATIONS PERSPECTIVE

FIGURE 4

MANAGEMENT REPORT EVALUATION FORM

---

**REPORTING SYSTEM EVALUATION**

APPRAISER_____

_____

REPORT NAME OR IDENTIFICATION: _____

_____

---

If your organization had to pay for this report, by obtaining it from a consultants firm, HOW MUCH WOULD YOU BE WILLING TO PAY:

- for the report as is             :$ _____
- for the report slightly modified as a result of your recommendations    : $ _____
- for the ideal report as you would design it          : $ _____

---

Express your opinion of the report.

Use the following seven point scale of opposite adjectives.

(check (✓) one space per line)

| | |
|---|---|
| good | bad |
| precious | common |
| important | unimportant |
| informative | uninformative |
| applicable | unapplicable |
| advantageous | harmful |
| reliable | unreliable |
| valuable | worthless |
| useful | useless |
| sufficiant | insufficiant |
| significant | insignificant |
| desirable | undesirable |
| necessary | unnecessary |
| pertinent | not pertinent |
| effective | ineffective |
| efficient | inefficiant |
| timely | ill timed |
| true | false |
| logical | illogical |
| readable | unreadable |
| clear | confusing |
| simple | complicated |
| ordered | disordered |
| precise | imprecise |
| complete | incomplete |
| up-to-date | out-of-date |

# CHAPTER 5

# The Transition To A More Human System

What can now be said of the human within the system? Ackoff (1971) suggested a way of seeing the human within as complex a system as an organization or an MIS. He presented three types of systems classified according to the behavior resulting from their internal and external events:[13]

1.  *The state-maintaining system* reacts in only one way to a different degree to any one of a series of events; always reacts in such a way as to maintain the same state or outcome; e.g., the thermostat, the governor of an engine.

2.  *The goal-seeking system* can respond differently to different or unchanged conditions to produce a desired result; can produce the same outcome in different ways; is self-learning and will produce the desired outcome more efficiently; cannot change its goal as a result of experience; e.g., automatic pilot.

3.  *The purposeful system*, goal-seeking, can produce a variety of outcomes under numerous conditions; can change its goal after acquiring experience; can change its methods of attaining a particular goal; the human being!

Prior to describing concrete design tools, it is essential that a link be established between the two systems, the human system and the information system. We may now refer to the *human information system*. Figure 5 (p. 35) is a schematic representation of the human being's information system as depicted from a description by K.J. Radford (1978). Read from left to right: data input, transmission to the nervous system, filtering by the synapses (contact points), insertion in memory, processing, and conversion of data into information, decision making and, finally, the communication of messages via the nervous system that enables the body to undertake actions. The following sequence is evident: data - information - decision - action. A highly logical sequence! A highly human sequence which will be more fully explored in Part II. It would appear that the human within the MIS is an *information system* within an *information system.*

The purpose of this section was to compare and equate the human information system and the organizational information system. Even though this examination is superficial, a striking resemblance appears between the two. Consequently, the efficient and effective design of an MIS implies a knowledge of the human within the system. How to acquire this knowledge and consider it in MIS design? An important fragment of the answer lies ahead.

# THE HUMAN BEING CONSIDERED

This book deals first with the human being - afterward, with information systems. To consider the members of an organization during the design of a Management Information System is not an easy task. Holmes (1970) identified a dozen factors that had to be examined to achieve a better MIS. On the one hand, he stressed the importance of top management's active involvement and support during the design stage and its ability to structure the MIS function. On the other hand, he stressed the importance of human relations. More recently, Radford (1978) developed prerequisites to a successful MIS:

1.  The system must be developed to respond to user needs. This includes design of output formats appropriate to each user level.

2.  Analysts and managers must cooperate in specifying detailed MIS requirements, based on the existing information system.

3.  MIS development is an evolutionary process, leading to flexibility

4.  MIS development is a project management effort, requiring that personnel be competent and that designers report directly to top management.

5.  The involvement of data processing is felt very early in the MIS design procedure.

6.  The most successful MIS implementation occurs when the acquisition, use, storage, and transmission of data and information are simplified and improved.

FIGURE 5

THE HUMAN INFORMATION SYSTEM

(Inspired from: Radford, K.J.,
*Information Systems for Strategic Decisions,*
Reston Publishing Company,
Reston, Virginia, 1978.)

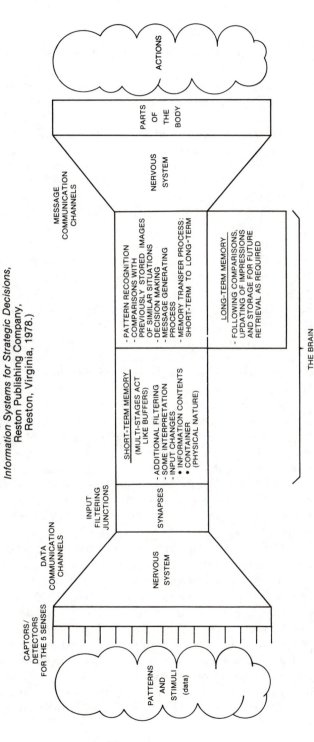

35

7. MIS outputs must be of appropriate format for the users.

8. An important consideration: MIS security and confidentiality.

Many of these factors refer directly to the human within the system. To consider the human requires a specific frame of mind on the part of everyone who will be included in the new design. I qualify this frame of mind or mental disposition as "Third Wave," from Alvin Toffler's revolutionary perceptions.

Toffler (1980) developed several key ideas about humans, their institutions, and change. In an article in *La Revue Commerce*, I isolated some of his ideas and oriented them toward the field of management (Hurtubise 1980). I identified lessons, suggestions, and directives, which can be used by managers who must live with, and in, the postindustrial era which is the third wave. To help you discover whether you are a third-wave manager, administrator, analyst, or secretary, I present a brief review of Toffler's ideas.

*Future Shock* by Toffler (1970), describes the trauma that affects both individuals and institutions accustomed to a low level of diversity and a slow tempo of change who suddenly must face high levels of diversity and rapid change. Whereas *Future Shock* presented mainly the processes which bring about this trauma, *The Third Wave* describes structures which enable one to live in the new era. These structures are exposed in terms of four integrated spheres: (1) the technosphere produces and distributes wealth; (2) the sociosphere assigns roles to individuals; (3) the psychosphere contains psychological indices; and (4) the infosphere produces and supplies information. These spheres belong to the third wave, a postindustrial era that differs significantly from its predecessors.

The first wave began at approximately 8000 B.C. and lost its momentum around 1650-1750 A.D. It was characterized by agricultural civilization, rural villages, and the general immobility of people.

The second wave, in which most of us were born, is marked by industrial civilization, huge cities, mobility, the corporation, and the notion of limited responsibility. The catalyst was the industrial revolution which achieved its apex between 1955 and 1965. The start of its decline can be traced to the creation of the Organization of Petroleum Exporting Countries. The public and private organizations of the industrial era have all borrowed much from the giant manufacturing organization: production on a repetitive basis, pyramidal structure, hierarchy of command, work division, unity of command, desire of managers not to transmit information, and decision-making under panic conditions. Six principles which apply equally to the socialist and capitalist camps define the parameters of the second wave:

- **Standardization** - of products,
- **Specialization** - leading to dehumanization,
- **Synchronization** - the "9 to 5" syndrome,
- **Concentration** - of work, effort, control
- **Maximization** - growth, gigantism, monopoly,
- **Centralization** - of methods and the *imperial presidency.*

The industrial era created the dichotomy of producers and consumers and the false association of men with the production function and of women with the consuming function. The leaders of this era can also be qualified as power technicians of an integrationist nature who run the machine in which an elite of generalists exercise a regulatory power on a subelite of specialists.

The third wave has been underway for approximately twenty-five years. This postindustrial era favors democratic decision-making processes and more direct participation by the consumer in the manufacturing process. It is the do-it-yourself era, the epoc of population dispersion and a critically increased reliance on information. Systems notions - systems theory - prevail.

Four groups of industries designate the third wave: electronics and data processing, space enterprises, oceanographic enterprises, and bio-industries (genetics engineering). With one exception (EDP), the technology of these groups is not yet widespread. In addition, the four structural spheres (techno, socio, psycho, and info spheres) overlap considerably in the new era.

The info-sphere, comprised of such concepts as *distributed computer processing, microcomputers, personal computers,* and *voice-activated terminals,* multiplies the means of communicating. It is responsible for the revolution in the factory and the office, the era of electronic mail and of the secretary who is increasingly involved in the organizational decision-making process. The third wave is also marked by work at home, part-time jobs, flextime, and the matrix organization. It is a demassified society in which the accent is placed on originality, diversity, and individual values and life styles. Therefore, the third wave requires a redefinition of the corporation, which, according to Toffler, will see several major changes imposed upon it. The physical environment will change and production will be reorganized in view of such key factors as energy availability, pollution, and consumer activism. The social milieu will see increased moral accountability, corporate ethics and social responsibility. The role of information will expand exponentially, expeically the exchange of information within organizations. And finally, the role of Government and of government agencies will also change.

The central theme of *The Third Wave* concerns the conflicting and tumultuous situations - of all kinds - which occur when many waves of change, none of which establishes predominance over the others, break upon society. The example is the American Civil War, which was fought to establish by whom the United States would be governed: the farmers (first wave) or the industrialists (second wave). Toffler contends that the decisive battle coming will be (perhaps already is) the one fought between those who attempt to maintain the industrial society and those who are already surpassing it. Change is inexorable.

# CREATIVITY AND CHANGE

The essential materials of the new era are creativity and change. For the manager, the theme can be interpreted as an imperative to create new types of organizational structures which utilize these essential ingredients. Two tests, one on creativity and one on third wave readiness, are presented in appendix A. In the text that follows, I will briefly describe the tests and what they measure. You may prefer, however, to detour immediately to the appendix to check your current creativity level and to see whether or not you are ready for the postindustrial era already upon us. Both tests are revealing and perhaps amusing. Remember that nothing is written in stone. We are each responsible for change. We start by changing ourselves, by learning not to close our minds prematurely to all that is new, surprising, and apparently revolutionary (Toffler 1980). What then are the tests and what do they reveal?

Eugene Randsepp of Princeton Creative Research designed the creativity test after isolating key characteristics of many highly creative people (Niles 1980). The test consists of seventy-four statements for each of which one of three responses is permitted: agree, in-between (or don't know), and disagree. Following the statements is a list of fifty-four adjectives from which the respondent is asked to select the ten that best describe her or him. Those who take the test are asked to answer as accurately and frankly as possible and to try not to guess how a creative person might respond. No time limit is imposed.

The answers to the test are assigned weighted values of that range from minus two to plus three, depending on the relative importance of the characteristic to either the inhibiting or the enhancing of creative processes. What was discovered?

Randsepp found that concentration, enthusiasm, reliance on intuition, a tendency to daydream, and aesthetic sensitivity were distinguishing attributes of the most creative people. Closely allied were dynamic curiosity, a sense of playfulness coupled with purpose-fullness, and initiative, self-assurance, and flexibility. On the other hand, the characteristics which tend to stunt creative processes included not only the opposites of those above, but also desires for certainty, order, the familiar, the rational, and clearcut roles. In short, no surprises.

Bearing a resemblance to the Delphi method of discussing ideas about the future and to the creativity test just described, the third-wave test checks one's readiness to participate in the postindustrial era. This test, too, was developed after studying the characteristics of a great number of highly third-wave people. Instructions for the fifty statements are the same as for the creativity test and a similar weighting system (on a scale of from minus three to plus three) is used to value responses.

Not surprisingly, many of the characteristics that are found most abundantly in creative people are found in the typical third-wave disposition. The keynotes are decentralization of control, a global perspective, acceptance and use of computer technology, democratized decision-making, and reliance on imagination. Conversely, the mark of a person who is determinedly of the second wave is precisely the status quo, that is, a yearning for the "good old days".

## IN SUMMARY

This ends my introduction to the systems approach and to the system of the future. The systems approach to complex phenomena is unique. In Part I, I exposed the system. In doing so, I provided an introduction to systems language and concepts. I differentiated between the scientific and the systems methods and their respective places in analyzing complex phenomena. I then developed the procedural steps and tools of systems analysis and, perhaps most importantly, defined information as distinct from data and data processing.

Now is the time of rapid change. I have highlighted several that impact most directly on organizational management, especially those relative to the new philosophy of accounting for the human within the system. I am looking at change and at structures and systems to enable us to live comfortably and effectively in the postindustrial era already upon us.

Part II will describe the Management Information System in full, a systems approach that permits the observation, analysis, evaluation, and modification of an organization within the context of its objectives - an invaluable tool indeed for management.

PART II

# AN MIS DESIGN PROCEDURE AND
## The Global Conceptual Framework

# CHAPTER 1

# The MIS Design Procedure: The Initial Phases

The procedure advocated for the design, development, and eventual installation of an MIS is inspired by Blumenthal (1969). This procedure emphasizes that problems related to MIS are less and less of the technical and data-processing variety, as was the case a few years ago. The problems or challenges are of the management and organizational kinds. Each of these phases will be thoroughly examined in this second part. For the moment, it is important to examine the types of people who will intervene in the procedure and to define their respective roles.

## WHO IS INVOLVED AND HOW?

**The Information Systems Analyst** — The examination of information needs involves a study of orientations and objectives and a justification of the organization's financial, human, and material resources. If success is gauged in terms of the system's acceptance, and use by its users, then the correct identification of user needs is a primary consideration. As a consequence, one of the first tasks of the information systems analyst is to identify what is expected of the system.

Unfortunately, because the expectations expressed by management are often nebulous the analyst usually avoids this step, neglecting to adequately search out the real reasons behind the desire by management to question their existing information system. In the following sections I will explain methods and techniques which will help the information analyst during this preliminary effort.

Another difficulty must be mentioned. Like all researchers, the information analyst risks being lured into a popular yet attractive trap — the temptation to seek out problems that coincide with his or her solutions! To avoid this bias, the analyst must eliminate thoughts of models, software, procedures, programs, and forms which seem initially to offer a perfect solution. Beware of easy and local solutions. An appropriate solution will be created only after the analyst is aware of the global reality which is the organization.

**The manager** is the MIS designer par excellence and plays the principal role. Like the analyst, however, the manager has particular ways of tackling problems. If the system is to achieve the ultimate aim for which it is built, namely to aid the decision-making processes, the manager, too, must avoid the easy and familiar way out.

Viewed in this light, the MIS can be both as sophisticated and as complex as desired. Yet it must still supply information to managers whose informational capacities are limited. Too often in this scenario managers, interrupted by telephone calls, colleagues, and subordinates, are additionally burdened with piles of computer listings. Information overload is a problem that results in a decrease in the capacity to make decisions.

In Part I, I examined the human being's decision-making process. All managers, when confronted with a decisional situation, tend to define the problem, generate alternative solutions and then choose between them. It is the decision maker who must identify the information needed for decisions. These needs, even if initially not as clear, rational, and logical as they could and will eventually be, constitute the very genesis of the design effort.

I have suggested that managers and analysts usually do not speak the same language. They perceive the world of the organization and its decision-making processes differently. Managers usually do not formulate the objectives they pursue, the criteria used to make decisions, nor the subsequent analysis of consequences in the same manner as would an analyst. How then to go about adequately determining and analyzing the information needs of management? There are many approaches. I will explore two.

A first approach is for the analyst to interview managers about their various responsibilities and decisions (Matthies 1977). In this manner, decisional situations which lead, for example, to investment decisions, expansion projects or budget control are explored. The result is a list of decisions belonging to different decision makers located at various organizational levels. It is then possible to establish the various information elements required to aid the decisions so identified. The obvious question which arises: Can the manager describe decision-making processes, responsibilities, and reference points which enable her or him to manage. How often we have heard analysts, after having spent hours and hours with a customer, exclaim, "She doesn't know what she wants." or "He's changed his mind again." On the other hand, many managers have expressed deep dissatisfaction with systems analysts and have exclaimed, "He doesn't understand anything." or "She just doesn't know how to listen."

A second approach concentrates the analysis on the organization: its structure and environment, its planning, supply, manufacturing, distribution, and control processes. The information analyst then acquires a global vision of an organization's characteristics from various sources, by observing, interviewing, and reading all relevant documentation. The basic danger inherent in this approach is that the analyst may be influenced by what the information needs are thought to be!

The first approach appears enticing because it involves interaction between analyst and manager in common quest. The second approach has the merit of being more operational. A question presents itself: Must we design personalized systems based on characteristics dependent on the decision maker's knowledge or on organizational structure, roles, and functions? And who decides?

*Participation*

As a general rule, all members of an organization must participate in the design of *their* MIS. Top management, however, is responsible for determining and clearly establishing who is to participate in the MIS design effort in general and in the MIS procedure in particular.

Occasionally top management considers hiring an expert. Why hire a consultant? Fried (1978) offered several major reasons. Because there is a shortage of skills in the marketplace, not every organization can have its own in-house specialist. Consultants bring the benefits of their broad exposure to information systems, objective viewpoint, and specialized skills. These specialists can save the executive time designing and implementing a system and by returning for intermittent needs that arise and training, or improving skills of, organizational members. Further, using outside consultants avoids salary inequities which could distort an organization's salary structure.

A systems team of MIS designers is the expert-consultant with specialized knowledge of systems analysis and design tools. The design team acts as a catalyst and offers a basis for comments and recommendations gathered not only from their own experience but also from all members of the organization.

We have stressed the importance of users' roles on a number of occasions throughout this book. Lucas (1974) was explicit in citing why future MIS users should participate in the design procedure:

Participation can be ego-enhancing, satisfying, and challenging, and results in a greater commitment to change. The creation of better solutions is effected because users are generally more knowledgeable about present operations and functions than are the systems design specialists. Lucas further suggested the creation of two committees:

1.  **A steering or priorities committee,** which includes members of top management, to help make resource allocation decisions thereby avoiding conflicts between system designers and eventual users. Both will have a better understanding of why certain projects are undertaken, why certain requests are denied, and why new applications and enhancements are chosen.
2.  **A design or user committee** which includes a large representative group of users and involves them in the design process. The net effect is manager-analyst-user interactions — a participatory design.

The message is clear. The success of the MIS procedure can be summarized in one word: *Participation*!

## THE DESIGN PROCEDURE

The *MIS procedure* is comprised of four phases:

PHASE  I  - The Plan's Goals and Rationales
PHASE  II  - Start With What Is: Document and Analyze the
                    Existing System
PHASE  III - The MIS Design and the Global Framework
PHASE  IV - Development, Exploitation, and Management.

## PHASE I — The Plan: Goals and Rationales

At the very beginning of the *MIS procedure*, a systems plan must be defined. The plan will constrain the behavior of that portion of the organization responsible for the design and implementation of specified subsystems. The subsystems will be guided by a strategic plan which will formulate objectives and allocate and conserve resources. The goal is to prolong the system's life and to make it more efficient. To this end, the plan will remain an initial plan. It will be flexible and indicate how to attain the goals related to a series of projects which will share available resources. This flexibility will also allow modification of the organization. That is, the new system will certainly impose changes.

The systems plan objectives have been well defined by Blumenthal (1969). A systems plan is elaborated to determine a reasonable sequence of development in terms of payoff potential, natural precedence, and probability of success. In avoiding unnecessary duplication of major systems elements which are applicable across organizational lines, and in reducing the total number of small, isolated systems to be developed, operated, and maintained, the plan minimizes the cost of integrating related systems. The system's plan also looks to the future. In laying a foundation for coordinated development of consistent and comprehensive, organization-wide and interorganizational information systems, the plan provides for adaptability of systems to organizational change and growth without periodic major overhaul. In addition, the plan establishes guidelines for and directions to continuing systems studies and projects.

## PRELIMINARY STUDY

More often than not, the systems plan in its initial version defines a preliminary study related to the MIS design effort. Usually the preliminary study is, in effect, a feasibility study whose objective consists in justifying a system in terms of its return on investment (Fried 1977). This objective notwithstanding, a preliminary study has a relative significance which depends on the scope of the initial systems plan and reflects top management's commitment. For instance, a preliminary study may establish the chances of success of the MIS effort within an organization. On the other hand, a preliminary study may imply a predesign of the future system.

## PLAN CONTENTS

An MIS systems plan, in its initial version, may be very short: a discussion of the participation and preliminary study issues. In its extended version, however, a plan as understood within the context of this book may refer to a number of topics. A full and complete MIS systems plan will:

1. Name the sponsor of the MIS concept

2. Summarize information management and MIS concepts and subconcepts as required

3. List the sectors involved in the MIS effort, including project boundaries and limits

4. Illustrate the relations between organizational objectives, strategies, and strategic attributes on the one hand and the MIS objectives, constraints, and design considerations on the other (King 1978),

5. Identify management and information subsystems involved in the design effort

6. Define the organization for the management of the information resource including: the mandate and composition of the design team and the creation of a unit responsible for information management and its relationship with other units

7. Create the position and define the functions of the information resource manager (Horton 1979)

8. Designate memberships in the steering and design committees

9. Schedule information sessions on the MIS project and training sessions for the MIS design team and for future users

10. Define the logical classification to be employed with the documentation, analysis and design forms[14]

11. Address such project management considerations as calendar, cost, training, etc

12. Provide for system evaluation and an exploratory cost/-benefit analysis (King and Schrems 1978).

## PHASE II — Start With What Is: Document and Analyze the Existing System

PHASE II of the MIS procedure requires, at the outset, documentation that can provide knowledge about the structure and functioning of the existing information system. This task will provide a basis or model for the design of the future MIS. The knowledge obtained may lead rapidly to the optimization of the existing system by identifying duplicate tasks and enabling the reduction of processing and communication delays.

Yvon and Semin (1970) suggest two methods for identifying and illustrating information flow circuits. The Natural Information Zones

Method literally follows the path taken by an element of data or information throughout the organizational units (individuals, divisions, services, departments, etc.). The Files Consolidation Method notes the inputs and outputs of each organizational unit. Both methods produce knowledge about data, processing, storage, communication, information, and the people involved with the existing information system.

Two principal documentation tools can be used: The visual representation panel and the data dictionary:

1. **The visual representation panel** illustrates the flow of data and information as well as their sources and destinations within an organization. It can depict processing, time delays, costs and organizational units at all stages of processing, transmission, and storage. This graphical representation is an excellent communication tool, for it provides a common language between managers and analysts.

2. **The data dictionary** identifies and characterizes all data, information, processing, users, and storage associated with the information system.[15] In its most primitive state, the data dictionary is simply a manually updated alphabetical list of data and information discovered during the documentation of the existing information system. In its most evolved state, it is a computer software package which can create a meta data base (data about data).

The data dictionary is a transitional tool. Its use does not end with the existing information system; it will be eventually used to document the data, processes, and information related to the new MIS.

In concluding the description of PHASE II, one final and essential remark is required. In this section we have not described a documentation form which could conceivably be used to gather all basic facts related to the existing information system. This form is, in fact, the one used to design the new information system - the MIS. This form, the documentation, analysis, and design form, will be thoroughly described in the following chapter.

*Phase* III is the *working* part of the MIS. In it we will describe a classification orientation for organizations, provide the theoretical background and develop a conceptual framework for the ensuing, fully elaborated MIS schema.

CHAPTER 2

# Phase III - The MIS Design and the Global Framework

PHASE III of the MIS design procedure is composed of three steps which will assign a logical classification to the organization, elaborate the conceptual bases for, and the actual design framework of, the MIS and elaborate the MIS schema.

## THE LOGICAL CLASSIFICATIONS OF THE ORGANIZATION

Many authors have developed approaches which permit the eventual design and development of a MIS. These so-called approaches are logical classifications. They define the departure point from which the appropriate MIS will be designed.

Blumenthal (1969) indicates how the design of the future system implies, on the one hand, a logical classification of the organization and, on the other hand, a basis for analysis and design - a conceptual design framework, a design on paper of the MIS. With respect to the first step he suggested six logical classification approaches:

1. **The data bank approach's** underlying theme is the establishment and maintenance of a vast pool of highly detailed data related to all aspects of the organization

2. **The data collection (bottom-up) approach** assumes that a system design is best accomplished after all the facfs have been assembled

3. **The management survey (top-down) approach** assumes that once the decision-making processes have been determined and the management information needs established, the subsystems necessary to supply the information can also be determined

4. **The organization chart approach** assumes that systems generally follow organizational boundaries. This approach permits the elimination of redundant data, information and activities from the various units. It tends to classify the organization in terms of its formal structure of positions, divisions, services, departments, sectors, etc

5. **The eventual integration approach** calls for continuing with design and implementation of individual systems as needed, without waiting for a comprehensive plan to be developed

6. **The total systems approach** is based upon the premise that all things between the organization and its environment are interrelated

A seventh classification approach, established by Yvon and Semin (1970), is related to the notion of data and information flow circuits and suggests the design of an MIS based on the information networks within the organization.

The seven above approaches can be regrouped into two categories (Longpré 1980). The data approaches include the first two and the configuration approaches include the last five. Thus, instead of speaking of seven classification approaches, it appears more appropriate to speak of two ambivalent approaches:

1. **The data analysis or modular approach** proceeds from the base of the organizational pyramid, classifies the organization in terms of operational modules and data bases, and suggests the development of an information system starting from the bottom and progressively filtering to the different decisional levels in the hierarchy

2. **The decision analysis or integrated approach** consists in classifying or viewing the organization from the point of view of information flow. This approach, proceeding from the summit, requires the analysis of objectives, resources, information needs, constraints, etc., and leads to the implementation of an information system oriented toward decision-making processes where system components are integrated

These two approaches - one structurally oriented, the other data oriented - blend together to help determine the information needs required to solve problems related to the management/decision complex. Where does one approach stop and the other begin? It is difficult to know what the exact proportion of these two approaches will be in any specific MIS design philosophy; that will be reflected by the use of the conceptual framework. One thing is certain: the ambivalence of the two approaches offers a flexibility which facilitates modification. It would seem also that these two ambivalent approaches are very close to the human within the system.

# CONCEPTUAL FRAMEWORKS: THEORETICAL FOUNDATIONS

A conceptual framework is a model on paper of the Management Information System. A framework is an inspiration for design, an aid to creative thinking. It is meant to help structure ideas related to the design effort, to facilitate communications between analysts and managers, to teach concepts about information systems, to provide a basis for resource allocations, to put designs and revisions into concrete form, and to suggest new directions for information systems research.

Perhaps a dozen frameworks for MIS design can be found in the management literature (Lucas, Clowes, Kaplan 1974). In this section we will examine eight. They will be presented in chronological order and identified according to their respective authors. The frameworks are:

1. Simon (1960)
2. Forrester (1961)
3. Dearden (1965)
4. Anthony (1965)
5. Blumenthal (1969)
6. Gorry and Scott Morton (1971)
7. Gerrity (1971)
8. Radford (1973)

*Simon's framework* is based on behavioral sciences and deals with problem-solving methods and techniques. There are two dimensions to this framework. The first divides problem solving into intelligence, design, choice, and review phases. The Intelligence phase surveys the environment and identifies conditions that require action. In the design phase options are developed for the situations identified during the previous phase. The Choice phase concerns the process of selecting a particular action from the set of options developed during the design phase, and in the review phase the past choices are assessed. The second dimension to Simon's framework divides decisions into two types: programmed (structured) and nonprogrammed (unstructured) (Table 3, p. 58).

*Forrester's framework* (1961) provides for understanding organizations through nonlinear feedback concepts as studied, for example, under the topic of control systems.[16] The information system and the decision-making process are viewed as the network-linking mechanisms that govern resource flows. Resources are system variables possessing two major characteristics: levels and rates of flow. Decisions regulate the rate at which levels change, from which resources originate and to which they are sent. The decision-making process is a response to the gap between organizational objectives and the progress made toward their attainment. Hence, the very logical sequence - Information - Decision - Action - that considers the global behavior of the organization and emphasizes information needs, decision-making, and objectives.

*Anthony's framework* (1965) is based on management accounting. The organizational pyramid, a direct result of the Anthony framework, describes three distinct types of decision activities in an organization and three corresponding types of information. Figure 6, (p. 57) inspired from an article describing the Gorry-Scott Morton framework (1971), summarizes in a schematic manner the elements of the Anthony framework.

Finally, a fourth level must be added to the three organizational levels. Of the transactions processing (question/answer) level Lucas (1976) notes:[17] "In one study of systems, it was not possible to classify systems completely according to the three types of decisions and their related levels of management described in the Anthony framework; instead, it was necessary to add a category below operational control decisions called *transaction processing.*"

*Dearden's framework* (1965) is applications oriented, dealing with the functional aspects of the organization and with computer technology. A vertical and horizontal categorization of functions are proposed: The horizontal classification deals with systems specification (decentralized tasks at the user level), data processing implementation (centralized tasks at the analyst level), and programming (centralized tasks at the group level). The vertical classification defines three major information systems - finances, personnel, and logistics.

*Blumenthal's framework* (1969) remedies the lack of consistency and uniformity which often occurs when related systems are integrated. The framework combines organizational units into a set of information, activity, and decisional subsystems. Blumenthal stresses that the planning and design of information systems should be based on such fundamental principles as the effective use of systems resources,

## FIGURE 6

## ANTHONY'S FRAMEWORK AND THE BASIC CHARACTERISTICS OF THE ORGANIZATIONAL PYRAMID

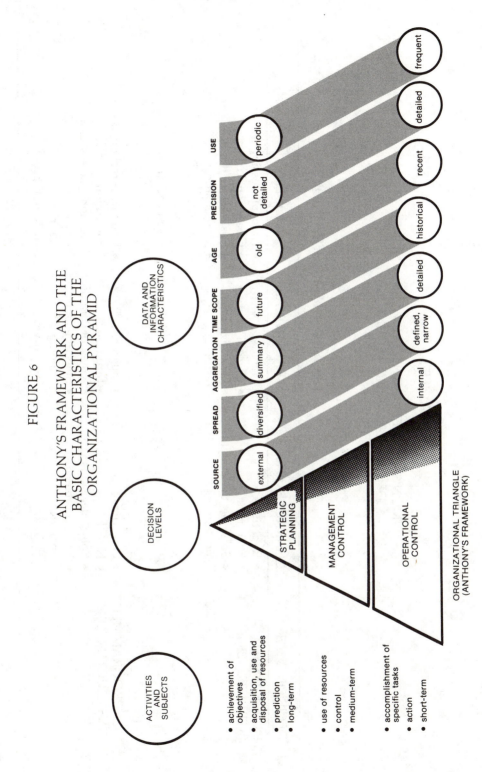

57

TABLE 3

SIMON'S CONCEPTUAL FRAMEWORK AND
DECISION-MAKING TECHNIQUES

DECISION-MAKING TECHNIQUES

| DECISION TYPE | CHARACTERISTICS | TRADITIONAL | MODERN |
|---|---|---|---|
| PROGRAMMED (STRUCTURED) | • Repetitive<br>• Routine<br>• Solvable by analytic procedures | • Habit<br>• Clerical routine<br>• Organizational structure | • Data processing<br>• Operations research<br>• Systems analysis<br>• Mathematical analysis<br>  - modeling<br>  - simulation |
| NONPROGRAMMED (UNSTRUCTURED) | • One time<br>• Novel<br>• Policy decisions<br>• Not solvable by analytic techniques | • Judgment<br>• Intuition<br>• Rules of thumb<br>• Selection and training of executives | • Heuristics techniques for training human decision makers and constructing heuristic computer programs |

efficiency in systems performance, systems life, and organizational change. The framework reduces the complex relationship that exists between various interconnections by grouping techniques. The elementary operational activities of an organization are grouped into separate, identifiable organizational entities such as activity centers and decision centers. These centers are then grouped by function and the resulting sets of groups defined as supporting each of three modules: operational control, management control, and operational information control. Blumenthal does not, however, address the decision-making structure related to the strategic planning level of the organization.

*The Gorry - Scott Morton framework* (1971), a synthesis of the work of Simon and of Anthony, classifies decisions in a two dimensional matrix where one axis refers to the organizational levels - operational control, management control and strategic planning - and the other axis establishes the structurability of decisions according to the classification: structured, semi-structured, and unstructured (Table 4, p. 60).

*The Gerrity framework* (1971) is oriented toward unstructed problems and decisions normally found at top management levels and emphasizes a *normative* model of the future system rather than the *descriptive* model of the actual system. The result of this framework, however, is a functional model, a compromise between the normative and descriptive models.

*Radford's framework*(1973), inspired by Dearden and by Anthony, suggests the division of the information system into five components: administrative and operational systems for routine functions, periodic management reports, common data base for use by more than one part of the organization, data retrieval system, and a data management system which structures and controls the flow of data among components of the information system.

## THE GLOBAL CONCEPTUAL FRAMEWORK

The design of a Management Information System may suggest the selection of one or more of the specific frameworks mentioned above. The concepts inherent to all of them are most valid and valuable during MIS design. Yet, because a number of them are rather theoretical in nature and present some problems concerning

TABLE 4

EXAMPLE OF THE GORRY - SCOTT MORTON FRAMEWORK

ORGANIZATIONAL LEVEL

| DECISION TYPE | STRATEGIC PLANNING | MANAGEMENT CONTROL | OPERATIONAL CONTROL |
|---|---|---|---|
| STRUCTURED | • Tanker fleet mix<br>• Warehouse location | • Budget<br>• Short-term forecasting | • Accounts receivable<br>• Order entry |
| SEMI-STRUCTURED | • New product introduction | • Variance analysis | • Inventory control<br>• Production scheduling |
| UNSTRUCTURED | • Research and development planning | • Personnel management | • Cash management |

their use in practice, a very real question presents itself: How to go about using the best of each?

In answer, I have developed the GLOBAL CONCEPTUAL FRAMEWORK, a concept which includes ideas belonging to the older frameworks. The global conceptual framework is practical in nature. It is destined for the manager-analyst team which, during an MIS design, must take into account a number of good theoretical ideas.

This MIS sequence of Data-Transformation-Information-Decision-Action can be interpreted as follows: Data that describe organizational phenomena (such as activities, tasks, functions) are transformed, either manually or automatically, into information contained in reports which are transmitted to decision makers. Decisions are made and corresponding actions carried out. The MIS sequence is looped by feedback which is capable of generating other data, transformation, information, decision, action - another MIS sequence. The global conceptual framework presented here enables the design, the identification, and the documentation of the set of sequences which will eventually constitute the organization's MIS.

Figure 7 (p. 62) is the didactic representation of the global conceptual framework. (I suggest the reader "paperclip" this figure for future reference). The framework is evolved by filling in the elements of a three-dimensional matrix. The columns and rows (vertical and horizontal axes) represent Gorry and Scott Morton's framework which is itself a synthesis of Simon's and of Anthony's frameworks.

In effect, the vertical axis is from Simon. Three levels of structurability — structured, semi-structured and unstructured — establish the degree of involvement of computer data processing. For example, a structured operation is amenable to computer processing, whereas an unstructured operation can be accomplished only by the human being.

The horizontal axis of the global framework depicts Anthony's organizational levels and Lucas' transaction-processing level. The levels indicated are: strategic planning (top management), management control (middle management), operational control (supervisory staff), and transactions processing.

The third axis is made-up of four tables (two-dimensional matrices) depicting Forrester's sequence of *information - decision - action* to which I have added *data*. These four tables represent the MIS sequences. The first table (farthest away in Figure 7) identifies data elements, the second illustrates information used by decision makers, the third indicates decisions, and the fourth notes the actions resulting from the decisions. This set of elements constitutes a

FIGURE 7

THE DIDACTIC REPRESENTATION OF
THE GLOBAL CONCEPTUAL FRAMEWORK

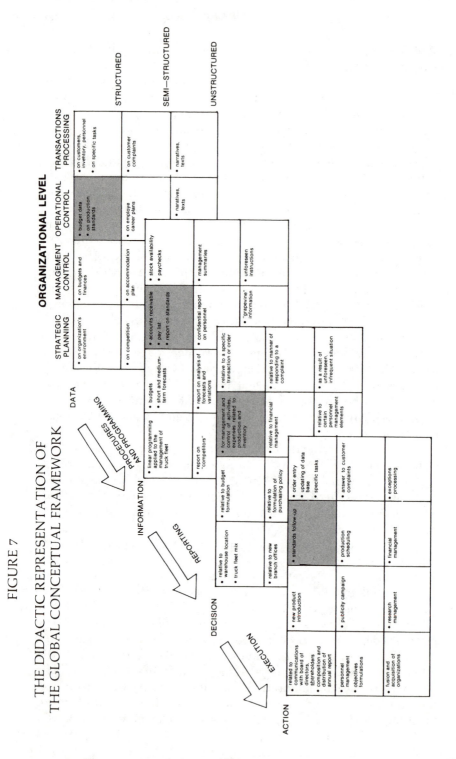

particular MIS sequence. I will follow through at one organizational level for a structured example. The structured-operational-control-compartment of the data table identifies budgeting and production standards. These data will be transformed (processed) by computer programs or by administrative manual procedures into information identified in the corresponding compartment of the information table as accounts receivable, pay list, and report on standards. This information is also contained in reports communicated to decision makers noted in the decision table. In this example, the situations noted refer to control of activities related to production and inventory. These identified decisions are executed as a standards follow-up as noted in the corresponding compartment of the action table.

The *MIS sequences* can be clearly visualized in the global conceptual framework. DATA are transformed by programs or procedures into INFORMATION contained in reports destined for decision makers who make DECISIONS which are then executed through specific ACTIONS.[18]

The global framework also includes other frameworks examined in the previous section (figure 8, p. 64). For those interested in further in-depth research, I have placed the author's name in parentheses after the applicable comment. First, the global framework refers to the possibility of considering such organizational sectors as personnel, finance, and logistics (Dearden).[19] Second, the separating of tables into the four following sets suggests a number of frameworks:

1. **The data bases set** is made up of all the data tables, identifies data elements, and suggests not only their grouping into records or common files, but also their structures within computer memory (Radford).

2. **The information reports set** is composed of all the information tables (Anthony).

3. **The decisions set** groups all the decision tables (Simon, and Gorry-Scott Morton).

4. **The actions/activities set** assembles all the action (activity) tables. (This set when linked to the decisions set not only translates but, to a great extent, simplifies the basic considerations found in Blumenthal's framework.)

Another use of the global conceptual framework is the illustration of the three models - *descriptive, normative* and *functional* (Gerrity).

FIGURE 8

THE GLOBAL CONCEPTUAL FRAMEWORK
AND ITS REPRESENTATION OF
ORGANIZATIONAL SECTORS AND THE ELEMENTS
OF THE MIS SEQUENCE

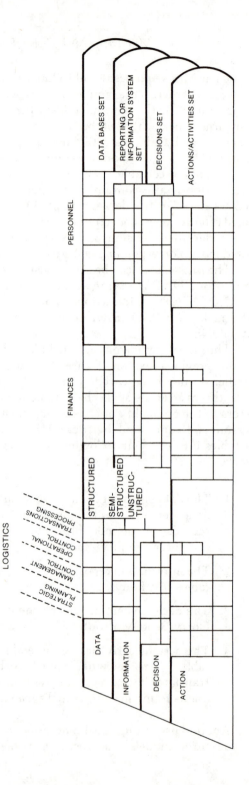

Figure 8 could thus reflect the sets associated with any one of these three models (remembering that the functional derives from the other two).

Each segment title (logistics, finances, personnel) could also be replaced by an option title. That is, the global conceptual framework can render the processes associated with the decision-making phases: intelligence on a system, design of system options, choice or selection, and review (control). The idea suggested is to design various system or subsystem options by using the global framework and, after subsequent evaluation, to select and retain the optimal MIS.

In closing this section on the *global conceptual framework*, a number of remarks - some short, some long - may be useful to the practitioner (the manager - analyst team) who would like to use this MIS design tool.

\* \* \*

**The logical classification of the organization.** Logical classification has been discussed. The ambivalent approaches, decision analysis, and data analysis, have been described. In effect, the sequence followed in order to fill in the tables of the global framework and its various compartments is dictated by the logical classification given to the organization at the start of PHASE III of the MIS procedure. Very simply, a *decision analysis* classification suggests that attention will center on upper organizational levels and that the decision table will be filled in first. On the other hand, a *data analysis* classification suggests that attention will center on lower organizational levels and that the data table will be filled in first. Ultimately, of course, all components will be completed.

\* \* \*

**Information reports and reporting structure.** Because information is a consequence of the MIS, the importance to be accorded to reports design and the reporting structure is evident. Knowledge gained and exposed in the global conceptual framework offers much in terms of an information report's contents and structure. Wilkinson (1976), in an excellent article, described three topics pertinent to the information reporting subsystem: report classification, report design considerations, and reporting structure.[20]

Report Classification

| Characteristics | Categories of reports |
|---|---|
| purpose | operating, control, planning, stewardship, legal compliance, motivational, proposal, action |
| scope | firm-wide, divisional, departmental, sales territory |
| conciseness | detailed, summary ("key item"), exception |
| occurrence | scheduled, periodic, on-demand, triggered |
| time horizon | historical, short-range forecast, long-range forecast |
| presentation | hard copy, soft copy (on computer display), oral presentation (with or without visual aids), narrative, graphical, tabular |
| user | management, owners, employees, governmental agencies |
| operating function | accounting, production, marketing |

Axioms of Report Design

1. A report should have a primary purpose and a scope that relates to the fulfilment of one of management's major responsibilities.
2. A report should be as concise as possible, providing information to users in a clear and readily usable format that is consistent with other reports generated by the firm.
3. A report should be issued in time to enable the manager to take effective action, should span an appropriate time period, and be discontinued when its cost exceeds its value.
4. A report should build upon input data derived from available sources and collected in sufficient variety and detail to provide the basis for adequate analysis.

Integrated Report Structure

| | |
|---|---|
| Top Level Managers (e.g., president, vice presidents, and managers of major functions) | - Narrative summary of current major projects and research programs<br>- Income statement, comparing budgeted with actual values<br>- Statement of profit earned by each product line and organizational segment<br>- Balance sheet, comparing last and current periods<br>- Cash flow statement, comparing projection with actual<br>- Control reports, comparing budgeted with actual expenses for each major unit and function<br>- Measures of key performance and success factors relating to entire firm and to major functions and divisions<br>- Long-range forecasts and planning reports, including relevant environmental information |
| Middle Level Managers (e.g., plant managers, division managers, purchasing agents, sales managers, chief accountants) | - Cost accounting operating summaries<br>- Statement of profit or loss (assuming of profit centers)<br>- Control reports. comparing budgeted with actual expenses for each department or cost activity at the lower levels<br>- Status or exception reports on inventories, maintenance, spoilage, product quality, idle time, facility utilization, personnel, etc.<br>- Measures of key performance factors relating to responsibilities<br>- Analyses of sales, orders, products, purchases, etc. |

|                          |                                                      |
|--------------------------|------------------------------------------------------|
|                          | - Medium-range planning reports and schedules        |
| Lower Level              | - Cost-accounting operating reports                  |
| (e.g., foremen,          |                                                      |
| supervisors,             | - Control reports, comparing budgeted with           |
| department               |   actual expenses                                    |
| heads, sales             | - Labor distribution and efficiency reports          |
| branch managers)         | - Measures of key performance factors relating to responsibilities |
|                          | - Short-range planning reports and schedules         |

\* \* \*

**MIS structurability.** The practical application of the global framework has required the formulation of functional definitions of the words *structured* (programmed), *semi-structured* (semiprogrammed) and *unstructured* (nonprogrammed) as they apply to the elements of the *MIS sequence.* As a result of this effort, a structurability hypothesis has been formulated which applies to every element of the sequence DATA - TRANSFORMATION - INFORMATION - DECISION - ACTION. The hypothesis: An element of the MIS sequence characterized by a certain structurability level cannot lead to a subsequent element whose structurability level is greater, *except for the decision element.* (See appendix B for a graphical illustration of this hypothesis for all three decision types.) In essence, a structured framework requires computer applications, an unstructured framework requires manual operations, and a semi-structured framework lies between these two and may use both or either.

\* \* \*

**Documentation discipline.** Aside from offering an efficient and sophisticated tool, the global conceptual framework imposes a discipline on the design, filling in all corresponding compartments and thereby completing all MIS sequences: data - transformation - information - decision - action.

\* \* \*

**Documentation precision.** The level of detail to be incorporated into the representation of the global conceptual framework is a function of the design objective. If a preliminary design is called for, only a general documentation is required. In the other extreme, a detailed design will require all of the conceptual facts, such as data elements and their sources, information report titles, contents and destinations, decision-making procedures, etc.

\* \* \*

**The semantics problem.** The use of the global conceptual framework requires an understanding of the future MIS users and, in essence, the language they speak. As a general rule, top and middle managers (strategic planning and management control) express themselves reasonably well in terms of the decisions they make and their decision-making processes. On the other hand, members of the other organizational levels (operational control and transaction processing) express themselves in terms of their actions, activities, tasks, responsibilities. An MIS can lead to a common language or, at the very least, translation capability.

\* \* \*

**Computer assisted design (CAD).** The inherent logic associated with the MIS sequence and the global conceptual framework suggests that the global framework should be inserted into a CAD system. Aside from establishing a dictionary of MIS sequence elements (data, transformation, information, decision, action), such a system would constitute a powerful analysis tool enabling the creation of relations and interrelations between various decision levels (strategic planning, management control, operational control, transaction processing) and the pre-defined and described elements. Such an instrument would assure a visible rationality and pertinence to the MIS design effort that would be felt right through to system implementation and all along the subsequent evolution of the organizational and informational structures. Such a system would also help establish and maintain the interrelationships between various information reports and organizational activities. It would contribute to their analysis and, more importantly, furnish an aid to the study of the organization's decision-making processes.

\* \* \*

**Visual representation of the global conceptual framework.** Although the didactic representation of the global framework (figure 7, p. 62) was conceived mainly for teaching purposes, it is used in practice. In fact, a number of visual representations have been developed and used by researchers, students, and practicing systems analysts in both the private and public sectors. The bank of case studies which have resulted confirms that the global conceptual framework is a powerful tool for the manager-analyst team.

Although no ideal visual representation exists, the author favors the representation of Figure 9 (p. 71). The level of detail suggests that representations of the various organizational levels can be aggregated and synthesized. For example, a set of representations of individual organizational positions can be summarized into a divisional representation; a divisional set can be summarized into a service representation; a service set into a departmental representation; and the set of departmental or functionl representations into a representation of the entire organization!

\* \* \*

*The office of the future* is, of course, encompassed by the *global conceptual framework*. The phrases "office of the future" or "office automation" generally and erroneously suggest word processing alone. Although the office of the future implies much more, the analyst using the global framework will correct three important misconceptions related to the use of word-processing equipment (Menkus 1981): Text processing is processing rather than communication oriented, text processing theory supposes that all documents produced are of equal value, and text processing is concerned with administrative costs rather than with the value of work produced. Office automation will have a real impact on an organization. There are many implications for future research. In an excellent article, Olson and Lucas Jr. (1982) developed research propositions which concern automated office systems. Viewed within the context of information management and system design, these propositions suggest concrete areas of study within any organization implementing office automation.

1. Automated office systems, especially text-processing functions, can improve the quality of written documents produced and can permit increased specialization of skills to support administrative and clerical tasks.

# FIGURE 9

## AUTHOR'S SUGGESTION OF VISUAL
## REPRESENTATION OF GLOBAL FRAMEWORK

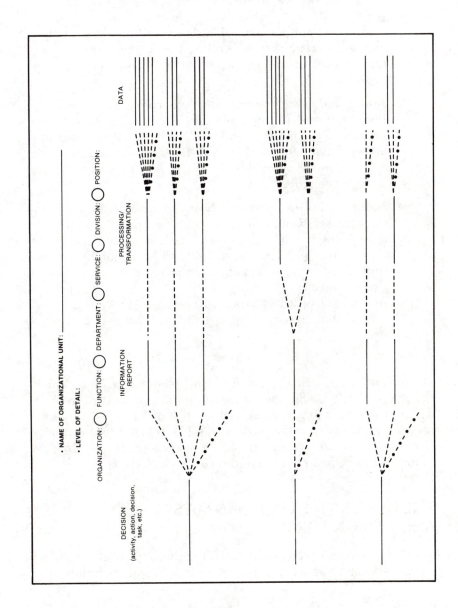

2.  Automated office systems, especially communications functions, can alter the physical and temporal boundaries of work, thereby affecting the degree of interdepartmental conflict and of perceived interdependence among departments.

3.  Automated office systems can affect the role identification, stress, and job satisfaction of office workers, especially clerical workers. Professional and managerial workers' feelings of identity with organizational goals and criteria for promotion may be affected, thereby altering the degree of interdepartmental conflict and of perceived interdependence among departments.

4.  Automated office systems, especially communications functions, can lead to improved efficiency and increased total volume of communication for all office employees, but to a decrease in the amount of face-to-face contact and a reduction in the quantity and quality of social interaction and reinforcement in the office.

5.  Automated office systems, especially communications functions and personal applications, can affect managers' perceptions of the degree of rationality, flexibility, and free space of their work, and can change methods for monitoring and controlling work. Automation can increase the span of manager's control.

6.  Automated office systems can improve the ability of the organization to accommodate structural changes.

\* \* \*

In conclusion, a final comment: The *global conceptual framework* is the principal MIS design tool. It is the thinking product of the MIS design effort that can be represented and shown "on paper". In short, the global conceptual framework serves TO JUSTIFY user information needs. It can pretend to do so - because of the decision rationalization effort required of the *manager-analyst team.*

# THE DOCUMENTATION, ANALYSIS, AND DESIGN FORM

Perhaps we have convinced the reader that the global conceptual framework can be used in practice to design a Management Information System and that it can serve the purpose of visualizing the MIS. However, how do we arrive at it? Obviously, the global framework is a finished product. How did it come about? The answer is simple and direct: by using another MIS tool, the documentation, analysis, and design form. It is a "work" tool which enables the determination of MIS sequence elements and their respective attributes. As illustrated in Figure 10 (p. 74), the form is made up of four sections corresponding to the MIS sequence: Organizational analysis, information reporting, processing/transformation, and data. ("Paperclip" this figure for later reference.) Column headings are defined as follows:

*Organizational Analysis Section*

Decisional Situation: Wording of a decision, activity, task, function, or responsibility of a set of these associated with an organizational position.

Intervening Position: Other position(s) implicated by or linked to the decisional situation; may intervene preceeding, following, during the decisional situation. The links established between such positions will be made clear when the documentation, analysis, and design forms for these positions have been filled in.

Periodicity/Frequency: The periodicity or frequency with which a decisional situation occurs.

Time: The time period related to the decisional situation.

Structurability: The decisional situation's structurability (very, semi or unstructured).

Catalyst:[21] An attention "grabber". The phenomenon which attracts the decision maker's attention and informs her or him that a decisional situation exists (for example, a directive from a superior, a customer order, the end of the month).

*Information Reporting Section*

Input (need): Information (need) originating from outside the position and used to undertake the decisional situation. The information report may consist of a memo, a statistical analysis, tables, graphics, telephone calls, narratives, oral presentation, etc.

73

FIGURE 10

# THE DOCUMENTATION, ANALYSIS, AND DESIGN FORM

**THE GLOBAL CONCEPTUAL FRAMEWORK**
DOCUMENTATION, ANALYSIS AND DESIGN FORM

PERSON/GROUP/POSITION INTERVIEWED _____
INTERVIEWER _____
DATE _____
FORM NO. _____ * Link to be established with other form

| ORGANIZATIONAL ANALYSIS | | | | | | | | INFORMATION REPORTING | | | | | | | |
|---|---|---|---|---|---|---|---|---|---|---|---|---|---|---|---|
| DECISIONAL SITUATION | INTERVENING POSITION* | | | PERIODICITY/FREQUENCY | TIME | STRUCTURABILITY | CATALYST | INPUT (need) | SOURCE* | INTERMEDIARY (need) | OUTPUT | DESTINATION* | PERIODICITY/FREQUENCY | STRUCTURABILITY | COMMUNICATION FORMAT/MEANS |
| | BEFORE | AFTER | DURING | | | | | | | | | | | | |
| 1 | | | | | | | | | | | | | | | |
| 2 | | | | | | | | | | | | | | | |
| 3 | | | | | | | | | | | | | | | |
| 4 | | | | | | | | | | | | | | | |
| 5 | | | | | | | | | | | | | | | |
| 6 | | | | | | | | | | | | | | | |
| 7 | | | | | | | | | | | | | | | |
| 8 | | | | | | | | | | | | | | | |
| 9 | | | | | | | | | | | | | | | |
| 10 | | | | | | | | | | | | | | | |
| 11 | | | | | | | | | | | | | | | |
| 12 | | | | | | | | | | | | | | | |
| 13 | | | | | | | | | | | | | | | |
| 14 | | | | | | | | | | | | | | | |
| 15 | | | | | | | | | | | | | | | |
| 16 | | | | | | | | | | | | | | | |

| PROCESSING/TRANSFORMATION | | | | | | | | DATA | | | |
|---|---|---|---|---|---|---|---|---|---|---|---|
| ADMINISTRATIVE/OPERATIONAL PROCEDURE (manual) | COMPUTER PROGRAM | INTERVENING POSITION* | TYPE | | | PERIODICITY/FREQUENCY | TIME | STRUCTURABILITY | DATA ELEMENT (indicate for "intermediary" and "input" information reporting only) | PERIODICITY/FREQUENCY | ENTRY SOURCE | STRUCTURABILITY |
| | | | REPORTING | COMPUTATION | UPDATING | | | | | | | |
| 1 | | | | | | | | | | | | |
| 2 | | | | | | | | | | | | |
| 3 | | | | | | | | | | | | |
| 4 | | | | | | | | | | | | |
| 5 | | | | | | | | | | | | |
| 6 | | | | | | | | | | | | |
| 7 | | | | | | | | | | | | |
| 8 | | | | | | | | | | | | |
| 9 | | | | | | | | | | | | |
| 10 | | | | | | | | | | | | |
| 11 | | | | | | | | | | | | |
| 12 | | | | | | | | | | | | |
| 13 | | | | | | | | | | | | |
| 14 | | | | | | | | | | | | |
| 15 | | | | | | | | | | | | |
| 16 | | | | | | | | | | | | |

Source: The organizational position from which the input originates.

Intermediary (need): Information locally created by the position in order to respond to the identified decisional situation. I refer here to personal data banks because the information is not communicated elsewhere.

Output: Information produced as a result of a decisional situation for other position(s) or for common storage (filing cabinet, computer data base, microfilm, etc.) and eventual use by other positions.

Destination: Position receiving or using the outputted information. Once again a link must be established with other forms, because what is an output for one position is an input for another.

Periodicity/Frequency: The frequency with which information reporting arrives at the position or is produced by it either as an intermediary or as an output.

Communication Format/Means: The formats and means used to communicate, such as narrative text, computer visual display or printout, telephone, oral presentation, drawing, visual panel, tabular, graphical representation, etc.).

*Processing/Transformation Section*

Administrative/Operational Procedure (manual): Refers to the manual processing of data by or for the position either to respond to the position's information needs (intermediary) or to respond to another position's information needs (output). Input data will be described on another form for the issuing source where it is identified as *output*.

Computer Program: The automatic processing of data by or for the position either to respond to the position's information needs (intermediary) or to respond to another position's information needs (output).

Intervening Position: An intervening position performing the processing/transformation; for example, the data processing center, a staff service, a clerk, etc. Another form describing another position will refer to the processing/transformation described.

Type: Three types of processing/transformation are possible: Reporting (report production, hard copy, soft copy, etc.), computation (statistical analyses, budgeting calculations, etc.) and updating of data.

*Data Section*

Data Element: The data element (or set of data elements) processed by or for the position. Only data processed or transformed for the production of intermediary and output reports are noted; data related to input reports are described in the form filled out for the source position.

Entry Source: The position (place) at which data entry is executed; for example, at the computer center, at the personnel department, etc.

Structurability: Structured data can be stored and retrieved from computer memory, whereas unstructured data usually require narrative texts which are better suited for storage and retrieval from manual filing systems; semi-structured data can be stored in a word-processing system.

Now that the documentation, analysis, and design form related to the global conceptual framework has been described, a how-to-use procedure may be forwarded. Table 5 (p. 77) is the practical procedure which aims at a high quality design defined by the future MIS users (Elam 1979). Again, the form is a work form from which the global framework will evolve. Initially, the documentation, analysis, and design form serves to document; afterward, it is used to analyze and design.

Finally, the logical classification (the ambivalent approaches of decision analysis and data analysis) applies to the documentation, analysis, and design form. Very simply, if a decision analysis classification is chosen, the Organizational Analysis and Information Reporting sections of the form are filled in first. On the other hand, if a data analysis classification is chosen then, the Processing/Transformation and Data sections be filled in first. A decision analysis classification further requires that the interview process begin with upper management levels, whereas a data analysis classification begins with members of lower organizational levels.

# THE MIS SCHEMA

In essence the MIS schema indicates a system's major features. The most concrete part of a MIS is a processing/transformation component which can take the form of a manual administrative/operational procedure or a computer program. These components are modules. An MIS is given structure by elaborating its modules —that is, by writing its procedures and programs.

Once the modules have been identified, their relationships are noted and they are grouped into subsystems. An MIS schema

# TABLE 5

## THE DOCUMENTATION, ANALYSIS,
## AND DESIGN FORM IN PRACTICE

1.  The analyst becomes familiar with the organizational positions and its members. Work descriptions may be useful; providing they are up to date!

2.  The analyst establishes a meeting agenda. A set of forms must be filled in for each person or group of persons occupying an organizational position.

3.  A first series of interviews is oriented toward the existing information system. The forms are filled in and draft copies are typed. The analyst then meets again with these persons and together they verify, correct, and analyze the forms describing the existing information system.

4.  A second series of interviews is oriented toward the MIS, the future system. The procedure to be followed is identical except the analyst now asks the persons interviewed to design the new system and to describe what the MIS should be. The analyst meets again with the interviewees and together they verify, correct, and analyze the forms describing the new information system, the MIS!

5.  Once all documentation, analysis and design forms of the various organizational positions have been collated, the manager-analyst team then elaborates the GLOBAL CONCEPTUAL FRAME-WORK which is the design on paper of the MIS.

indicates the manner in which modules are grouped together to form subsystems and how these subsystems are themselves linked together and to the rest of the organization. For instance, if an analysis reveals that a data base sector is updated by one module and used by another, the second module could not function without the first. Therefore, it is important that a schema illustrate this type of functional particularity. Also, a schema should indicate the periodicity/ frequency of processing (daily, weekly, on demand, etc.) by the individual modules as well as their geographical distribution (thereby evaluating the need for the use of telecommunications, teleprocessing, main-frame computers, minicomputers, terminals, etc.). Although certain very specialized activities are generally not included, a schema should indicate certain technical priorities and, in doing so, distinguish between stable elements of operational processing control and variable elements of information management reporting.

The reader will recall that during PHASE II of the design procedure, analysis of the existing information system, the visualisation-representation panel and the data dictionary constituted important documentation tools. These tools can still illustrate, define, and document the new information system. A complete schema will include at a minimum: program and subsystem descriptions, decision tables and flowcharts, data and information descriptions, and procedural and operational considerations.

The objective of a complete system documentation is to describe in sufficient detail the system which responds to MIS user needs. These documents are prepared by the information analyst working under the supervision of the manager-analyst team. They are an adjunct to the visual representation panel and the data dictionary.

An MIS conceptual framework is distinct from an MIS schema. The conceptual framework is the thinking part of the information system design effort. It represents and presents MIS design in its purest sense; it justifies the future users' information needs. On the other hand, the schema is the execution part of the MIS design. It illustrates the production of information for various system users. Very simply, the conceptual framework answers the question: Why? and the schema answers the question: How?

# AN APPLICATION: THE FICTITIOUS ORGANIZATION

In the previous sections a number of tools useful to MIS design were presented. The object of this section is to illustrate the use of these tools by referring to a fictitious organization (Hurtubise, 1981). This section is intended - as is every other portion of this book - for both the manager and the analyst. Two illustrations demonstrate how, in practice, an organizational MIS is designed.

In figure 11 (p. 83) simplified organizational chart of a fictitious organization is noted by seven positions (A to G), distributed according to four levels: strategic planning, management control, operational control and transaction processing, and three sectors: personnel, accounting and sales. ("Paperclip" this figure for later reference.)

*The logical classification*

I choose a data analysis approach (bottom-up), an approach initially centered on the organization's lower levels and on data and their processing which enables the eventual filling in of all the columns of the documentation, analysis, and design form.

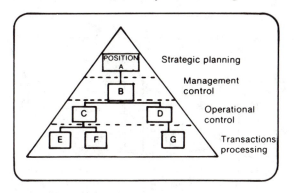

*The documentation, analysis, and design form*

For present purposes, a simplified version of the form is used and constitutes the design departure point of figure 11. To appreciate its use and the significance of the column headings, a narrative description of each organizational position is provided. The reader is invited to follow line by line on the figure.

**Position E** (a personnel clerk): A decisional situation (a decision, task, or objective) numbered 02 requires an information report numbered R03 which is intermediary to the position, that is — it does not come from nor will it be transmitted to another position. This is a computer report resulting from the processing of data contained in personnel form numbered F02. Position E also produces an information report, numbered R04, which is an output to position C. Again, report R04 is produced by computer programs which call on data contained in personnel form F02.

**Position F** (an accounting clerk): This decisional situation is numbered 01 and an intermediary information report, R01, produced by computer, is required and will be used solely by position F. The corresponding accounting data are contained in form F01. Position F also produces report, R02, for position C. This report is computer produced as a result of the processing of the contents of form F01.

**Position G** (a salesclerk): The decisional situation is numbered 04. The clerk manually produces, by an operational procedure, information report R07, which is forwarded to position D. The data processed to produce this report are contained in sales form F03 which, let us imagine, is filled in by the organization's sales representatives.

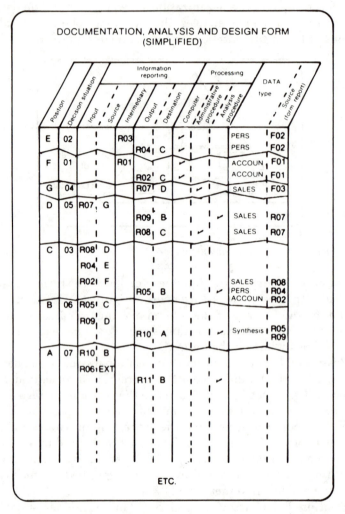

**Position D** (the sales manager): The decisional situation is identified by the number 05. Three reports are associated with this position. First, position D receives, as an input, report R07 from position G. Also, position D produces two reports: R09, a sales analysis and summary (forthcoming from sales report R07) which is communicated to position B; and R08, produced by an administrative procedure (using data from sales report R07) which is communicated to position C.

**Position C** (the accounting and personnel manager): The decisional situation is identified as 03. C receives three information reports (three inputs) and produces one output report. The input reports have already been identified: Report R08 originates from position F (accounting). The output report R05 is comunicated to position B. This report is a synthesis of sales - personnel - accounting.

**Position B** (the vice-president): The decisional situation is 06. This position receives two reports, one communicated by position C (report R05) and one by position D (report R09). The analysis and synthesis of these two reports generates information report R10 which is communicated to position A.

**Position A** (the head of the organization): The decisional situation is 07. "A" receives not only information report R10- from position B, but also report R06 from an exterior regulatory agency. Position A produces an output, report R11, which is communicated to position B.

In the foregoing exercise a form was filled in for each organizational position. In this simplified example, only one decisional situation was identified for each of the seven positions. In the real world, a number of decisional situations are associated with each organizational position. Each one, along with the corresponding information reports, corresponding processing, etc., will be identified on the documentation, analysis, and design form.

*The global conceptual framework*

As illustrated, the documentation, analysis, and design form is essentially a work tool used initially as a documentation form. To clearly represent the contents of the various forms I use a visual representation tool - the global conceptual framework. The framework, also illustrated in figure 11 (p. 83), is a transposition of the contents of the documentation, analysis, and design forms. A link must be established between the copies of the form and the framework.

In figure 11 (p. 83), three tables are located beneath the title *Global conceptual framework*. A first table shows the decisional situations of the seven organizational positions, a second table indicates the information reports belonging to those positions, and a third is related to the data entry function. Other tables could have been constructed to represent, for example, the processing transformations (the computer programs and the administrative procedures). What is important here is to represent the structurability of the three elements: decisional situation, information report, and data.

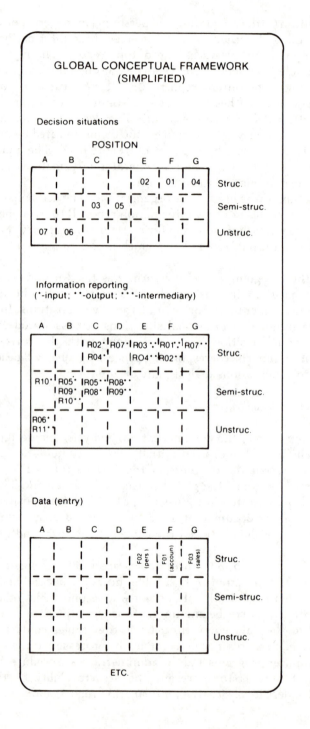

GLOBAL CONCEPTUAL FRAMEWORK
(SIMPLIFIED)

Decision situations

POSITION

|   | A | B | C | D | E | F | G |   |
|---|---|---|---|---|---|---|---|---|
|   |   |   |   |   | 02 | 01 | 04 | Struc. |
|   |   |   | 03 | 05 |   |   |   | Semi-struc. |
|   | 07 | 06 |   |   |   |   |   | Unstruc. |

Information reporting
(ˉ-input; ˉˉ-output; ˉˉˉ-intermediary)

|   | A | B | C | D | E | F | G |   |
|---|---|---|---|---|---|---|---|---|
|   |   |   | R02ˉ R04ˉ | R07ˉ | R03ˉˉˉ RO4ˉˉ | R01ˉˉˉ R02ˉ ˉ | R07ˉˉ | Struc. |
|   | R10ˉ | R05ˉ R09ˉ R10ˉˉ | R05ˉ R08ˉ | R08ˉˉ R09ˉˉ |   |   |   | Semi-struc. |
|   | R06ˉ R11ˉˉ |   |   |   |   |   |   | Unstruc. |

Data (entry)

|   | A | B | C | D | E | F | G |   |
|---|---|---|---|---|---|---|---|---|
|   |   |   |   |   | F02 (pers ) | F01 (accoun) | F03 (sales) | Struc. |
|   |   |   |   |   |   |   |   | Semi-struc. |
|   |   |   |   |   |   |   |   | Unstruc. |

ETC.

# FIGURE 11

## AN ORGANIZATION: THE DOCUMENTATION, ANALYSIS, AND DESIGN FORM, AND THE GLOBAL CONCEPTUAL FRAMEWORK

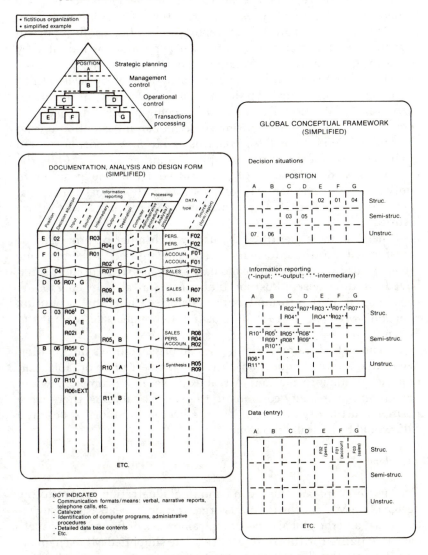

The first table identifies decisional situations 02, 01 and 04, belonging to positions E, F and G, respectively. The situations are structured and can be accomplished by routine and sequential procedures. On the other hand, decisional situation 07 of position A and 06 of position B are unstructured and require the capabilities and

83

resources of top management levels. Finally, decisional situations 03 (position C) and 05 (position D) are qualified as semi-structured.

Information reports are also seen in the global conceptual framework of figure 11 (p. 83) as a function of position (columns) and structurability (rows). Each report is classified as an input, an output, or an intermediary for a particular position (as indicated by the asterisks). In the information reports table, the structured reports can be produced by computer programs or by well-defined administrative procedures. For instance, the structured row identifies reports R02, R04, R07, R03 and R01 as being of this category. The semi-structured reports requiring some human intervention during their production include R10, R05, R09 and R08. A report outputted from a position must become an input to another position. Only the intermediary reports are not transmitted from one position to another. This particular way of illustrating the global conceptual framework assures that all information reports are used, that all are justified.

The final table identifies the data which must be processed or transformed into the information reports identified in the previous table. In this example, all data and data entry are structured (It could have been otherwise.): Position E obtains data related to personnel (form F02, P. 152), position F obtains data regarding the accounting function (form F01, p. 151) and position G obtains sales data (form F03, p. 153).

A conceptual framework justifies an organization's information needs. It answers the question: Why do members of an organization require specific information? A real example, more complex, would have required as many columns to the various tables as there were positions in the organization. Yet the procedural tools to design a MIS would be basically the same.

*The schema*

Figure 12 (p. 86), the second and final illustration related to the design of an MIS for the fictitious organization, repeats the organization chart and the global conceptual framework of figure 11. ("paper-clip" this figure for future reference). The simplified MIS schema is also illustrated. Like the framework, the schema is a visualization tool. The schema, however, represents the production of information or the various transformations of data into information reports. A schema answers the questions: How? Where? Who? How many? How much? When?

We have designed a system that is a mix of computer and manual data processing. In the same manner that a link was established between the documentation, analysis and design forms and the global conceptual framework of figure 11,(p. 83 ), a link will be established between the global framework and the schema of figure 12, (p. 86).

To begin with, the computer data processing part of the schema illustrates that position E uses a VDT to enter personnel data from form F02 and position F enters accounting data from form F01. In this manner the computer memory or data base is supplied and updated with data.

The computer is then used to produce four information reports: The R03 intermediary report for position E, the R01 intermediary report for position F, and the R04 and R02 reports inputted to position C.

The manual side of the system should also be noted in the schema of figure 12 (p. 86). The system designer has opted to manually process the data related to the organization's sales sector (even though these data are structured - as indicated in the data table of the global framework). Notably, it is position G who is responsible for sales data entry (form F03 is used); the given data are stored in a manual data base (such as a filing cabinet). G then processes data manually to produce report R07 for position D, who uses this input to produce, in turn, two information reports: First an analysis and synthesis of report R07 to produce report R09 for position B, and second, a procedure to produce report R08 for position C.

Position C analyzes and synthesizes manual report R08 and two computer reports, R04 and R02. The resulting product, report R05, is communicated to position B. Position B then analyzes R05 along with R09 (received from position D) and effects a synthesis, report R10, which is transmitted to position A. Finally, position A, who also receives R06 from outside the organization, analyzes and synthesizes both to produce R11 which is communicated to position B.

This is the end of the narrative description of figures 11 (p. 83) and 12 (p. 86) as they relate to the fictitious organization.

## CONCLUSION

Figure 13 (p. 87) summarizes four major tools examined in this chapter. They are, in order of use: the logical classification approach; the documentation, analysis, and design form; the global conceptual framework; and the schema.

The use of these tools has been illustrated with a simplified example belonging to what has been qualified as a fictitious organi-

# FIGURE 12

## AN ORGANIZATION, THE GLOBAL CONCEPTUAL FRAMEWORK, AND THE MIS SCHEMA

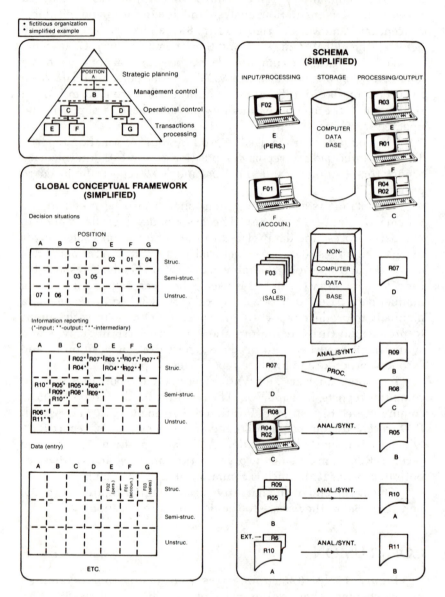

zation. However, does it not seem familiar? Although simplified, does it not resemble your department? Your business? Your hospital, school, or organization?

# FIGURE 13

## FOUR PRINCIPAL MIS DESIGN TOOLS

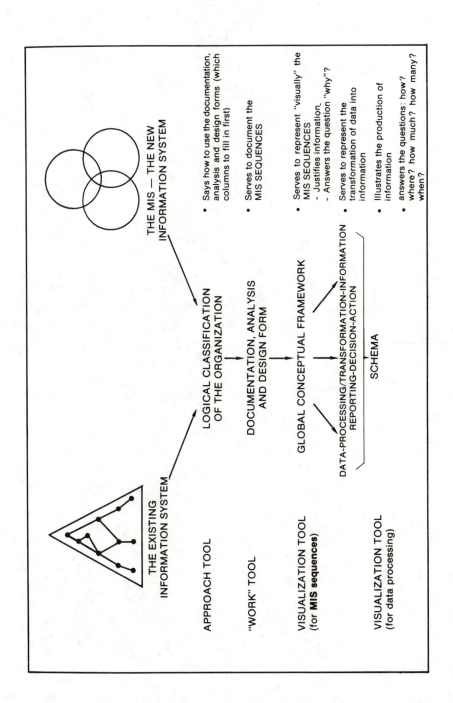

# CHAPTER 3

# In Search of a More Human MIS

In the previous chapter a number of MIS design tools were examined. These tools indirectly considered the human within the system. Can we consider the human within the system in a more direct manner?

Some authors have dealt with the human element in MIS design, addressing particularly the office environment and activities in a physical sense, and considering such items as lighting, acoustics, work station design, office layout, and human/computer interfaces. These human elements are important. One has only to think of the ever-increasing use of visual display terminals to be convinced of the importance of such details as screen color, image crispness, message format, and response time (Galitz 1980). Our approach to dealing with the human within the system will differ from the physical check-list approach, but will be just as specific and factual.

In a discussion on the future of information systems concepts, Mason and Mitroff (1973) elaborated five principal design variables (note that at least three are human oriented):

## Psychological type

- Thinking-sensation
- Thinking-intuition
- Feeling-sensation
- Feeling-intuition

## Class of problems

- Structured
  - Decisions under certainty
  - Decisions under risk
  - Decisions under uncertainty
- Unstructured - "wicked" decision problems

### Inquiring Systems (IS) — Method and guarantor of evidence generation

- Lockean (data based)
- Leibnitzian (model based)
- Kantian (multiple models)
- Hegelian (deadly enemy-conflicting models)
- Singerian-Churchmanian (learning systems)

### Organizational context

- Strategic planning
- Management control
- Operational control

### Modes of presentation

- Personalistic
  - Drama-role plays
  - Art-graphics
  - One-to-one contact group interaction
- Impersonalistic
  - Company reports
  - Abstract models-computerized information systems

There are a number of articles which have dealt with the human variable. Some attempt to familiarize the analyst with design considerations based on the MIS user by presenting results of empirical studies and by offering lists of ideas, suggestions, and rules.[22] For instance, Argyris (1971), in a famous and often quoted article, referred to the principle sources of user resistance to MIS. Carper (1977) added to these considerations by listing causes of resistance: threat to one's status or power; to one's ego; economic security; feelings of insecurity; uncertainty or unfamiliarity; increase in job complexity; changed relationships between superiors and subordinates; job or role ambiguity; job rigidity and time pressures and, finally, changed interpersonal relationships and work patterns. He also suggested that these causes could be diminished by, (1) clear and precise objectives, (2) user-oriented design, (3) top management involvement, (4) participatory design methods, (5) atmosphere favoring change, and (6) appreciation of the social consequences of the future system and of human communications.

The fundamental question remains: To achieve a modern MIS design, is it possible to consider the human within the system in a more formal way? Have we solved sufficient technical problems related to MIS development that we may now undertake a design study which will concretely consider certain behavioral aspects of such a system? For instance, how are the decision makers' psychological and cognitive types to be included in the design?

This chapter will suggest a new practical orientation to the design of Management Information Systems. The global conceptual framework and the documentation, analysis, and design form described will be expanded.

The missing link, the forgotten entity, in MIS design is the user.[23]

To answer the question of how to concretely consider the human within the system, three humanization tools are proposed (Voyer and Hurtubise 1979). They refer to the organization's decision-making processes, the MIS users' psychological and cognitive styles, and the MIS designers' inquiring systems (Hurtubise 1981).

## HUMANIZATION TOOLS

### The Decision-Making Processes

Organizational decision-making processes have been described, and generalized models of these processes have been elaborated. The models are not perfect, but one model is particularly powerful. We refer to the work accomplished by Vroom and Yetton (1973), and Jago (1974).[24]

The decision processes, styles, or situations defined by these researchers require that the decision maker have some area of discretion in determining the solution adopted, and that the solution affect at least one of the decision maker's subordinates. A fundamental dichotomy exists: Individual decisions, where the options retained affect but one subordinate, and group decisions, where the options retained affect all immediate subordinates or some readily identifiable subset of them.[25] The decision processes according to Vroom, Yetton, and Jago are the following:

1. **For individual decisions** (option retained affects one subordinate):

    Autocratic-I:  You solve the problem or make the decision yourself, using information available to you at the time.

Autocratic-II: You obtain necessary information from the subordinate, then decide on the solution to the problem. You may or may not tell the subordinate what the problem is. The subordinates role is clearly one of providing specific information, rather than generating or evaluating alternative solutions.

Consultative-I: You share the problem with the relevant subordinate, getting his or her ideas and suggestions. Then you make the decision, which may or may not reflect your subordinate's influence.

Group-I: You share the problem with one of your subordinates, analyzing the problem together to arrive at a mutually satisfactory solution in an atmosphere of open exchange of information and ideas, and contributing toward resolution with relative contributions that are dependent on knowledge rather than formal authority.

Delegated-I: You delegate the problem to one of your subordinates, providing him or her with any relevant information you possess, but giving him or her responsibility and support for solving the problem alone.

2. **For group decisions** (the option retained has potential influence on all or an identifiable subset of subordinates):

Autocratic-I: (same as for individual decisions)

Autocratic-II: (same as for individual decisions)

Consultative-I: (similar to individual decisions) Subordinates are not brought together as a group.

Consultative-II: You share the problem with your subordinates in a group meeting. In this meeting you obtain their ideas and suggestions. Then, you make the decision which may or may not reflect their influence.

Group-II: You share the problem with your subordinates as a group. Together you generate and evaluate alternatives and attempt to reach concensus on a solution. Your role is that of facilitator, coordinating the discussion, keeping it focused on the problem, and making sure that the critical issues are discussed. You do not try to influence the group to your solution, and you will accept and implement any solution which has the support of the entire group.

The Vroom, Yetton, and Jago model recognizes that in the real world of the organization, ten general decision situations exist, five are termed individual decisions and five are termed group decision. The model is, in fact, a normative model of decision processes which enables the evaluation of a particular decision situation and its classification according to the ten decision styles or processes. Figure 14 (p. 94) is a decision tree of the processes identified in the normative model. To use it, start at the left-hand side of the tree and work toward the right-hand side, asking eight questions, requiring a Yes or No answer. The eight questions that follow correspond to the eight letters, A to H of figure 14.

A. Is there a quality requirement such that one solution is likely to be more rational than another?

B. Do I have sufficient information to make a high quality decision?

C. Is the problem structured?

D. Is acceptance of the decision by subordinates critical to effective implementation?

E. If I were to make the decision by myself, is it reasonably certain that it would be accepted by my subordinates?

F. Do subordinates share the organizational goals to be attained in solving this problem?

G. Is conflict likely among subordinates over the preferred solutions? (irrelevant in individual problems.)

H. Do subordinates have sufficient information to make a high quality decision?[26]

FIGURE 14

THE DECISION TREE FOR THE VROOM,
YETTON, AND JAGO NORMATIVE MODEL

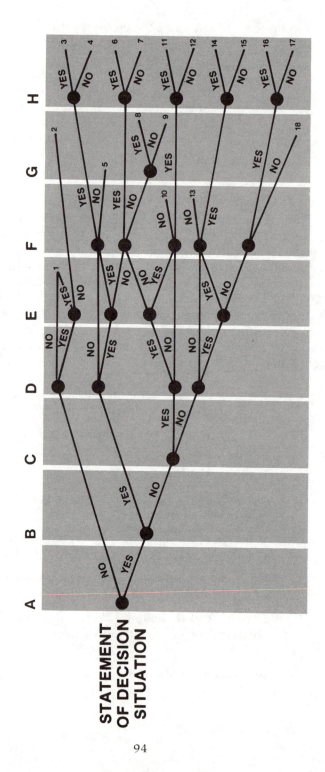

STATEMENT
OF DECISION
SITUATION

## TABLE 6

### THE DECISION PROCESSES OF THE VROOM, YETTON, AND JAGO NORMATIVE MODEL

| CODE NUMBERS* | CATEGORY | DECISION STYLE |
|---|---|---|
| 1 | GROUP | ALL |
| | INDIVIDUAL | ALL |
| 2 | GROUP | GROUP-II |
| | INDIVIDUAL | GROUP-I DELEGATED-I |
| 3 | GROUP | ALL |
| | INDIVIDUAL | ALL |
| 4 | GROUP | ALL |
| | INDIVIDUAL | ALL except DELEGATED-I |
| 5 | GROUP | ALL except GROUP-II |
| | INDIVIDUAL | AUTOCRATIC-I AUTOCRATIC-II CONSULTATIVE-I |
| 6 | GROUP | GROUP-II |
| | INDIVIDUAL | GROUP-I DELEGATED-I |
| 7 | GROUP | GROUP-II |
| | INDIVIDUAL | GROUP-I |

| 8 | GROUP | CONSULTATIVE-II |
|---|---|---|
| | INDIVIDUAL | CONSULTATIVE GROUP-I |
| 9 | GROUP | CONSULTATIVE-I CONSULTATIVE-II |
| | INDIVIDUAL | CONSULTATIVE-I GROUP-I |
| 10 | GROUP | AUTOCRATIC-II CONSULTATIVE-I CONSULTATIVE-II |
| | INDIVIDUAL | AUTOCRATIC-II CONSULTATIVE-I |
| 11 | GROUP | ALL except AUTOCRATIC-I |
| | INDIVIDUAL | ALL except AUTOCRATIC-I |
| 12 | GROUP | ALL except AUTOCRATIC-I |
| | INDIVIDUAL | AUTOCRATIC-II CONSULTATIVE-I GROUP I |
| 13 | GROUP | CONSULTATIVE-II |
| | INDIVIDUAL | CON SULTATIVE-I |
| 14 | GROUP | CONSULTATIVE-II GROUP-II |
| | INDIVIDUAL | CONSULTATIVE-I GROUP-I DELEGATED-I |
| 15 | GROUP | CONSULTATIVE-II GROUP-II |
| | INDIVIDUAL | CONSULTATIVE-I GROUP-I |

| 16 | GROUP | GROUP-II |
| | INDIVIDUAL | GROUP-I |
| | | DELEGATED-I |
| 17 | GROUP | GROUP-II |
| | INDIVIDUAL | GROUP-I |
| 18 | GROUP | CONSULTATIVE-II |
| | INDIVIDUAL | CONSULTATIVE-I |
| | | GROUP-I |

---

* Corresponding to the decision tree for figure 14, p. 94. Note the hierarchy of receiving reports for decisional situations is as follows: for Autocratic I — only the decision maker; for Autocratic II — first subordinate, who then communicates information to decision maker; for both types of Consultative and Group — decision maker and subordinate(s) simultaneously; and for Delegated — decision maker alerted, then subordinate receives report.

When a terminal node is reached, a code number (1 to 18) designates the decision category (individual or group) and one or more decision-making processes considered appropriate for the decision. The numbers are noted in Table 6 (p. 95) and identify the corresponding decision processes. Whenever more than one appropriate decision process is offered as possible options, one must be chosen. How? Perhaps by considering two factors. The first is the time available for decision-making. When time is limited, processes like Autocratic and Delegated may be most appropriate. The second factor considers training subordinates. The personal and professional development of subordinates suggests the use of participatory processes such as Consultative and Group.

Within the context of the global conceptual framework a model such as Vroom, Yetton, and Jago's is an important aid to the rationalization of decisional situations; it helps identify *who* must receive information on a decisional situation. For example, a situation employing the Autocratic-I process means that only the decision maker involved receive the associated information. On the other hand, a situation employing the Autocratic-II process suggests that both the decision maker and her or his subordinate(s) receive the related information. Consultative-I and II and Group-I and II also imply that both receive pertinent information reports. Finally, one design interpretation of Delegated-I would be that the MIS alert the decision maker of an impending decisional situation. It would then act as the catalyst or attention grabber referred to on the decision, analysis, and design form. Once the decision maker has subsequently *delegated* the decisional responsibility, the MIS would inform the chosen subordinate. Table 7 (p. 99) presents the author's opinion on information report receptors as a function of the decision-making process.

The forms appendix contains a figure (form-1, p. 151) that is an adjunct to the global conceptual framework and to its documentation, analysis and design form (figure 10, p. 74). It relates the decisional situations identified to one of the ten decision processes of the Vroom, Yetton and Jago model. This form adds to the rationalization effort associated with the organization's decisional situations in two ways: First, by identifying the members of an organization involved with and required by each decisional situation and, secondly, by determining the recipients of corresponding information reports. It may even suggest the quantity or volume of information to be transmitted to the decision maker and to his or her subordinate(s).

## Psychological and Cognitive Types

An important variable which must be considered in designing a more human MIS is directly related to the principal interested party -the user. This variable significantly affects the MIS design and its effectiveness. Chances of success are appreciably increased by adapting the communication and presentation of reporting to the user's psychological and cognitive style.[27]

Carl Jung devised a classification method of psychological and cognitive types. Figure 15 (p. 100) shows a simplified model of Jung's typology. There are two axes:

1. **The vertical perception axis** on which two means, sensing and intuition, permit the human being to obtain data from the world. "Sensing" suggests the use of the senses to gather facts related to decisional situations. "Intuition", on the other hand, suggests significations and relations which go beyond the senses. Human beings generally use a combination of these means of perception but tend also to lean toward or prefer one more than the other.

2. **The horizontal judgement axis** on which two means, thinking and feeling, permit the human being to decide. "Thinking" implies a

TABLE 7

THE RECEPTORS OF INFORMATION REPORTS
FOR A DECISIONAL SITUATION
AS A FUNCTION OF DECISION MAKING PROCESS

| DECISION PROCESS | RECEPTOR(S) OF INFORMATION REPORTS FOR A DECISIONAL SITUATION |
|---|---|
| AUTOCRATIC-I | only the decision maker |
| AUTOCRATIC-II | first the subordinate who afterwards communicates the information reports to the decision maker |
| CONSULTATIVE-I | the decision maker and the subordinate simultaneously |
| GROUP-I | the decision maker and the subordinate simultaneously |
| DELEGATED-I | the decision maker is first informed of the decisional situation (attention catalyzer), then the subordinate receives complete information reports |
| AUTOCRATIC-I | only the decision maker |
| AUTOCRATIC-II | first the subordinates who afterwards communicate the information reports to the decision maker |
| CONSULTATIVE-I | the decision maker and the subordinates simultaneously |
| CONSULTATIVE-II | the decision maker and the subordinates simultaneously |
| GROUP-II | the decision maker and the subordinates simultaneously |

INDIVIDUAL DECISIONS
(where the option retained affects but one subordinate)

GROUP DECISIONS
(where the option retained affects all subordinates)

# Figure 15

## Simplified Theoretical Model of Carl Jung's Typology

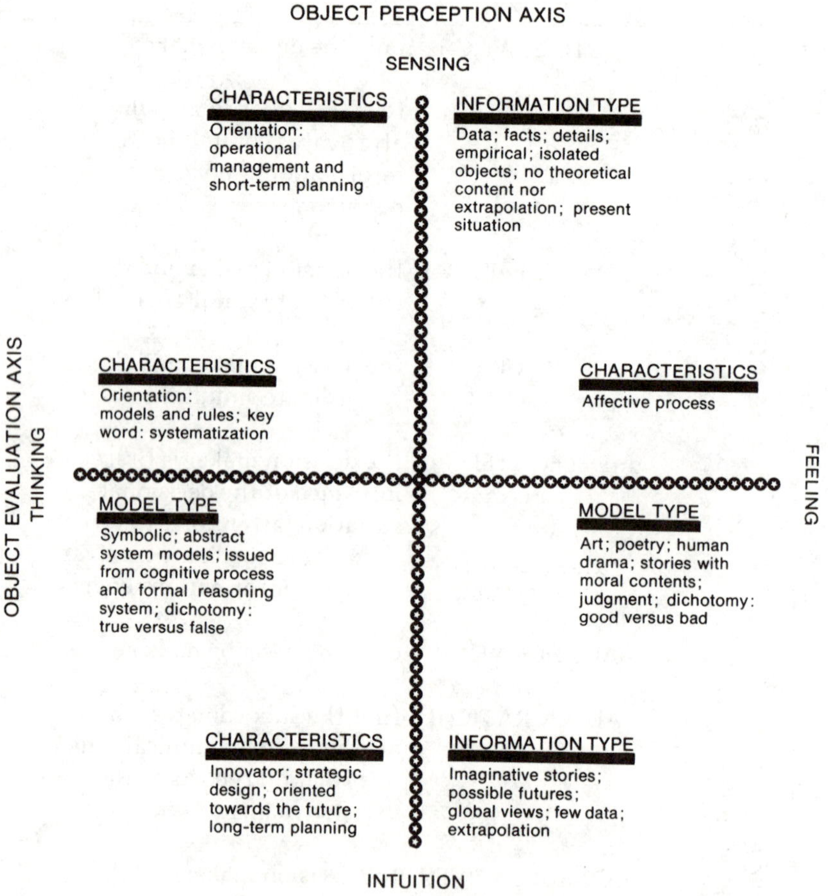

OBJECT PERCEPTION AXIS

SENSING

**CHARACTERISTICS**

Orientation:
operational
management and
short-term planning

**INFORMATION TYPE**

Data; facts; details;
empirical; isolated
objects; no theoretical
content nor
extrapolation; present
situation

**CHARACTERISTICS**

Orientation:
models and rules; key
word: systematization

**CHARACTERISTICS**

Affective process

OBJECT EVALUATION AXIS

THINKING

FEELING

**MODEL TYPE**

Symbolic; abstract
system models; issued
from cognitive process
and formal reasoning
system; dichotomy:
true versus false

**MODEL TYPE**

Art; poetry; human
drama; stories with
moral contents;
judgment; dichotomy:
good versus bad

**CHARACTERISTICS**

Innovator; strategic
design; oriented
towards the future;
long-term planning

**INFORMATION TYPE**

Imaginative stories;
possible futures;
global views; few data;
extrapolation

INTUITION

logical sequence that results in a decision. "Feeling" refers to personal values associated with the decision making process. Again, humans use and are affected by both but tend toward one or the other.

Different combinations of perception and judgement preferences produce different sets of interests, needs, and habits. Each combination also determines to a great extent how an individual gathers and appraises information.

A "sensing-plus-thinking" person is mainly interested in facts (collected by the senses) which can be verified. Decision making is thus based on facts and is effected by neutral and impersonal analyses characterized by a systematic reasoning process. A "sensing-plus-feeling" person is also interested in facts, but makes decisions with personal warmth because personal values are considered. For this reason an "intuition-plus-feeling" person also makes decision with personal warmth but is interested not so much in cold facts as by different and new possibilities (new products, new projects, new truths). The "intuition-plus-thinking" person is interested in new possibilities and approaches, these with impersonal analyses because she or he prefers thinking.

A number of tests measure human behavior.[28] The Briggs Myers and Briggs test (1962, 1979) for the identification of psychological and cognitive types is popular. The Myers-Briggs indicator situates an individual on the sensing-intuition axis and on the thinking-feeling axis. Myers-Briggs posits an important thesis of "mutual usefulness of opposite types." Thus, the intuitive type needs the sensing type to remind him to verify facts, to recall them, and to keep track of detail. The sensing type needs the intuition type - to see possibilities, to forward new ideas, to explain complex phenomena. Similarly, the thinking type needs the feeling type - to persuade, conciliate, forecast, teach, and sell. The feeling type needs the thinking type - to analyze, organize, find errors, and follow rules and policies.

The Myers-Briggs indicator also measures two other variables (not directly included in this discussion but which might be of interest to the reader) that can be associated with an individual and with her or his psychological and cognitive type. An extroversion-introversion variable indicates to what extent an individual is outwardly or inwardly oriented, and a judgment-perception variable indicates to what degree an individual uses perception and judgment while interacting with the outside world. There is no bad or incorrect psychological and cognitive type. All are good. All are human!

Psychological and cognitive types can be linked to the design of the MIS. Such knowledge will certainly inform the designer of the means and formats required to best represent the information reporting that the user may require. Nutt (1979) defined four types of decision makers. Each corresponds to the four psychological types just enumerated:

1.  The **systematic** decision maker - **sensing plus thinking** type

    • structures decisions by elaborating a plan to evaluate data

    • has confidence in data evaluation, indicates choices and bases decisions on evaluation results

    • stresses hard data and logical analysis

    • devises rules that govern the decision process

    • verifies data

    • prefers a centralized organization, well-defined authority and stresses profitability or financial viability, and

    • prefers defining roles, assigning work, and pushing for results

2.  The **judicial** decision maker - **sensing plus feeling** type

    • relies on consensus to dictate a course of action

    • disregards general issues

    • focuses on human relations that influence choice and describes these relation by facts

    • seeks quantitative information but processes it with a decision group

    • prefers a decentralized organization with clear-cut roles and work rules, and

    • stresses participative decision-making

3.  The **intuitive** decision maker - **intuition plus feeling** type

    • relies on unverbalized hunches or cues

    • disdains data

    • relies on the big picture

    • believes in social responsibility and quality-of-life considerations

- believes decision impossible without considering context

- views models as unable to capture the complexity of important decisions

- considers the human element

- prefers adaptive decision models

- prefers decentralized organization with delegation of authority

- relies on the advice of trusted peers, and

- believes that leadership stems from charisma

4.  The **speculative** decision maker - **intuition plus thinking** type

    - logically analyses data depicting hypothetical possibilities

    - elaborates formal plan based on contextual factors

    - devises several premises and tests them through analysis

    - evaluates performance with respect to own criteria

    - poses what-if questions

    - has an ability to define problems

    - prefers liaison rather than power centers

    - offers leadership through example, and

    - prefers combining evaluations of both objective and subjective data

The MIS designer should be able to identify the psychological and cognitive types of information system users and should be able to consider two very essential design elements: Information report *formats* and communication *means*. Table 8 (p. 104) presents an hypothesis on information report formatting and communication or transmission means. The preferential formats that should be given to reports and the preferential means for communicating their informational contents are indicated in accordance with P.C. Nutt's (and, indirectly, Briggs Myers') classification of the decision maker (Lusk and Kersnick 1979).[29]

The forms appendix contains a figure (form-2 p. 152) that adds (once again) to the global conceptual framework and to its documentation, analysis, and design form (figure 10, p. 74). It relates

# TABLE 8

## MIS DESIGN CONSIDERATIONS:
## INFORMATION REPORTING AS A FUNCTION OF
## USER PSYCHOLOGICAL AND COGNITIVE TYPES

| DECISION MAKER TYPE | PREFERRED FORMAT | INFORMATION REPORT PREFERRED COMMUNICATION MEANS |
|---|---|---|
| SYSTEMATIC (sensing-thinking) | tabular/ graphical | textual (hard copy: computer listing, etc., or soft copy visual display) |
| JUDICIAL (sensing-feeling) | graphical/ tabular | verbal (oral) |
| INTUITIVE (intuition-feeling) | narrative | verbal |
| SPECULATIVE (intuition-thinking) | narrative | mix of textual and verbal |

each decision maker or MIS user to a psychological and cognitive type as identified by the Myers-Briggs indicator.

In closing this discussion on psychological and cognitive types as they relate to MIS users, it is well to emphasize that there are many other avenues of research on the subject matter. Two will be briefly mentioned. First, Kolb's (1974) learning styles and processes related to problem solving. As is the case with psychological and cognitive types, it is possible to establish an individual's learning style. Standards exist, as do accompanying learning style tests.

The second avenue of research is Lafontaine and Lessoil's work on *visual* and *auditive* types.[30] Lafontaine's theory classifies an individual according to visual or auditive sensorial affinities. The difference depends upon whether a person uses eyes or ears predominately to become acquainted with new situations. The visual is concrete, interested in detail, has a photographic type memory, prefers drawings and schemas, and is quantity oriented. The auditive seeks the global and abstract view, has a listening type memory, enjoys texts and technical files, and is quality oriented. On this matter, it is interesting to read a citation attributed to Peter Drucker (Gabarro and Kotter 1980).

> Subordinates can adjust their styles in response to their bosses' preferred method for receiving information. Peter Drucker divides bosses into "listeners" and "readers". Some bosses like to get information in report form so that they can read and study it. Others work better with information and reports presented in person so that they can ask questions. As Drucker points out, the implications are obvious. If your boss is a listener, you brief . . . in person, then follow it up with a memo. If your boss is a reader, you cover important items or proposals in a memo or report, then discuss them . . .

## Designer Types — The Inquiring Systems

The psychological and cognitive type was associated with Management Information System users. What of the system's designer? This subsection will adress the MIS designer . . . whoever he or she is. The MIS designer will be classified according to type of inquiring system. This seems to better describe her or his manner of contribution, much as the psychological and cognitive types better described the user variable.[31]

The notion of inquiring systems is attributed to Churchman (1971). This behavioral orientation greatly influences the MIS designer's design and will greatly influence the analysis conducted, the design created and, finally, the MIS developed. As was the case for psychological and cognitive types, there is no bad inquiring system. *A priori* knowledge of the preferential inquiring system which makes up the designer's behavioral fabric can be very revealing and useful. Churchman identified five inquiring systems, which he named after five well-known philosophers. The analyst or designer types classified according to the five inquiring systems are:[32]

1. Gottfried Wilhelm Leibniz (1646-1716), the German philosopher and mathematician who invented one of the first microcomputers, the calculating machine. His major literary work, *Monadology* (1714), expresses his idealistic philosophy. The *Leibnizian* analyst is interested in rational, abstract, and deductive models, believes that truth is analytical and can be represented by a rational model, searches for a purely rational justification for the basis of a proposition or affirmation, and questions the precision and certainty of results.

2. John Locke (1632-1704) was an English philosopher for whom the source of knowledge was located in experience whereby sensation is combined with reflection. The *Lockean* analyst considers data prior to the development of formal theories or models, likes to observe and to analyze results, searches without creating a formal model or attempting to justify an assertion, feels that objective data, consensus of some group of experts, and supporting statistics are important.

3. Emmanual Kant (1724-1804), a German philosopher, was the idealistic critic for whom things as such are unknowable; they become known as phenomena, providing they cross the space-time continuum and that we become aware of them. The *Kantian* analyst believes that models and data are inseparable and is interested in a combination of data and models which best satisfy the given objectives.

4. Friedrich Hegel (1770-1831), the German philosopher, identified the human being and human thought as a function of the idea that develops according to the sequence, thesis - antithesis - synthesis. The *Hegelian* analyst is oriented toward a dialectal synthesis of two or more different models, and estimates that truth can be discovered through a state of conflict and a subsequent agreement. In considering that every set of propositions is a reflection of a more general plan about the nature of the world as a global system, the Hegelian searches for a differing global view that would permit the serious consideration of a completely opposite set of propositions. The conflict between a plan and its counterplan generates a third plan or global view that is a creative synthesis of the original two.

5. E.A. Singer, Jr., the American philosopher, invented and described the *sweeping-in* concept whereby one converges toward the

solution to a problem. The *Singerian* analyst believes that truth is pragmatic and all possible means must be used to understand a problem. This type recognizes that the analyst is part of the system. He or she approaches the basic problem with as broad a perspective as possible, making sure that the correct questions are asked and that the right objectives are identified and emphasized. The Singerian pursues a converging process that specifically recognizes bias of the analyst.

The preceding list also progresses from the less to the more *difficult* problems that are less and less structured. But how does a systems designer establish if he or she is Leibnizian, Lockean, Kantian, Hegelian, or Singerian?

The essential differences among the five types are concerned with preferences in world view and with approaches to problem solving. A test, "System Designers, Who Are You?" (Hurtubise 1983), helps determine designer type or combination of types. In essence the various types bear striking similarities to Jung's psychological and cognitive types by which we characterized users and to Nutt's decision-maker types. See Appendix C (p. 145) for the test. Here we will but describe each type and the combinations that most frequently occur.

*The Pure Leibnizian* seeks purely rational justifications, uses rational models as the basis of propositions, and perceives theory as critical to the attainment of analytical truth. This type always asks how one has arrived at a position, insists on deductive reasoning and relies very heavily on data precision. The interests of a modern Leibnizian include operations research, queuing theory, inventory control, and computer simulation.

*The Pure Lockean* observes and compares assertions to reality, questioning the probability of each assertion's correctness. Preferring data over models, the Lockean uses inductive reasoning to study data collected, which, when objective, become the justification for assertions. Both the Leibnizian and the Lockean prefer structured problems and systematic, step-by-step approaches to dichotomous ends. That is, they both seek a yes/no or true/false end. Gray areas or fuzziness are problematic.

*The Pure Kantian* believes that data and models are inseparable, considers either data or models first, depending on the problem, and creates models of possible solutions. In searching for a combination of data and theory justification, the Kantian applies her or his belief in truth through theory and through empiricism. This type is open to alternatives, seeks multiple views to promote solution, prefers semi-structured problems, and is interested in cost-benefit analyses.

*The Pure Hegelian*, preferring a global and dialectic view, looks for opposing views, seeking truth through a synthesis of differing models or opposing views. This type accepts, even welcomes, conflict of opinions and ideas.

*The Pure Singerian* seeks the broadest view, asking whether the correct questions are being asked, and whether the best or most useful objectives are being sought. A pragmatist, the Singerian prefers the brainstorming approach and recognizes that the designer is very much a part of the system designed. Solutions, therefore, reflect the personality and the biases of the solver. The Singerian is intuitive and accepts the validity of any means of understanding a problem. Both the Hegelian and Singerian prefer unstructured problems, distrust theory alone to account for reality, and can work easily with nonobjective, nonrational persons.

Although we have seen that decision processes and psychological and cognitive types could be directly considered in MIS design, this is not necessarily the case for inquiring systems. The management-analyst team must be acutely sensitive to the particular circumstances of its environment and have a heightened consciousness of the myriad design possibilities within it. One can presume for instance, that to this day most Management Information Systems have been designed and developed by Leibnizian analysts using models first, and by Lockean analysts using data first. In the future more and more MIS designs will be accomplished by the Kantian analyst who considers that models and data are inseparable, by the Hegelian analyst who seeks a synthesis of contradictory system plans, and by the Singerian analyst's pragmatic way of converging toward a system solution. Also, more and more semi- and unstructured decisional situations will be considered and included in MIS designs.

The last figure in the forms appendix (form-3 p. 153) completes -for the last time in this book - the documentation, analysis, and design form of the global conceptual framework. It attempts to identify the inquiring system(s) favored by member(s) of the MIS design team.

## APPLYING HUMANIZATION TO THE MIS

This book's goal is ambitious: the integration of the human element into the design framework of Management Information

Systems (MIS). What this book proposes is no less than the first outline of what can become a humanization theory for information systems.

In the preceding pages I have presented various concepts and tools related to MIS design and development. I have also designed an information system for a simplified and fictitious organization. As a result of my continuing research, much has been accomplished since that case study was composed. To illustrate recent practical analyses and designs undertaken in real organizations, I will demonstrate MIS humanization with a fictitious example that is not so fictitious.

Figures 11 (p. 83) and 12 (p. 86) illustrated the design effort principally oriented toward the use of the four major design tools: (1) the logical classification approach, (2) the documentation, analysis, and design form, (3) the global conceptual framework, and (4) the schema.

The reader will recall that seven decisional situations had been noted, one for each organizational position. Table 9 (p. 110) describes these decisional situations and links them to each of the seven positions (A to G). The upper organizational levels of this example deal with activities more complex than those associated with lower levels.

Eleven reports (R01 to R11) and three forms (F01, F02 and F03) were identified. Table 10 (p. 111) describes the information reports and relates them to the seven organizational positions (A-G) and to their respective decisional situations. Information reports are classified as either *inputs, outputs* or *intermediaries*. There is an obvious sequence to the elaboration of information reports. Lower organizational levels (E,F and G) collect data via the three forms F01, F02 and F03. These data are then processed (either by computer or manually) and refined, eventually becoming information useful to the decision makers who occupy positions A, B, C and D and their decisional situations. Therefore, table 10 represents what has been illustrated in figures 11 (p. 83) and 12 (p. 86) but names have now been given to the three forms and to the eleven reports. This MIS design had not directly considered information system humanization as developed in this chapter. We will now undertake a more human design by considering the three following variables:

1. Decision-making processes.

2. MIS user psychological and cognitive types.

3. MIS designer inquiring systems.

TABLE 9

THE DECISIONAL SITUATIONS OF
THE ORGANIZATIONAL POSITIONS
DESCRIBED IN FIGURES 11 AND 12

| | | DECISIONAL SITUATION |
| Position | Number | DESCRIPTION |
| --- | --- | --- |
| A | 07 | organizational development plan |
| B | 06 | personnel evaluation and assignment |
| C | 03 | personnel performance rating |
| D | 05 | sales performance |
| E | 02 | daily operational processing of personnel data |
| F | 01 | daily operational processing of accounting data |
| G | 04 | daily operational processing of sales data |

## Decision-Making Process

The Vroom, Yetton, and Jago model of decision-making processes was studied in a previous section. Those people within the organization that will receive the reports can make an important contribution to the MIS design of the first humanization variable and should be included in the process. Corresponding to each of the ten decision-making processes are information report receptors. Table 11 (p. 113) relates this hypothesis to the simplified organization as an example. It reveals analysis results which enabled the establishment of particular decision-making processes and the identification of the organizational positions acting as information report receptors. Four of the seven decisional situations have been analyzed according to the eight questions of the decision tree (figure 14, p. 94), and the corresponding decision processes (table 6, p. 95).[33] Referring to the table 11, I note:

1. A's decisional situation, *Organizational development plan* (07), is a group decision involving a number of subordinates in which only one decision-making process is possible: GROUP-II, which means that positions A, B, C, and D become the simultaneous receptors of the two input information reports noted in table 10: organizational status (R10) and economic context by region (R06).

110

## TABLE 10

### INFORMATION REPORTS RELATED TO
### THE DECISIONAL SITUATIONS OF TABLE 9

| | INPUT REPORTS | | | INTERMEDIARY REPORTS | | OUTPUT REPORTS | | |
| POSITION | NUMBER | SOURCE | DOC. NAME | NO. | DESCRIPTION | NO. | DESTI-NATION | DESCRIPTION |
|---|---|---|---|---|---|---|---|---|
| A | R10 | B | - organizational status | | | R11 | B | - organizational development plan |
| | R06 | external | - economic context by region | | | | | |
| B | R05 | C | - financial and personnel status | | | R10 | A | - organizational status |
| | R09 | D | - sales analysis | | | | | |
| | R08 | D | - sales statistics | | | | | |
| | R04 | E | - personnel presence | | | | | |
| | R02 | F | - statement of accounts | | | | | |
| C | | | | | | R05 | B | - financial and personnel status |
| D | R07 | G | - sales statistics | | | R09 | B | - sales analysis |
| | | | | | | R08 | C | - sales statistics |
| E | F02 | employee | - employee time card | R03 | - employee description card | R04 | C | - personnel presence |
| F | F01 | employee | - invoice check | R01 | - sales register | R02 | C | - statement of accounts |
| G | F03 | employee | - sales list | | | R07 | D | - sales statistics |

2. B's decisional situation, *Personnel evaluation and assignment* (06), is a group decision for which the model permits all decision-making processes but retains CONSULTATIVE-I.[34] Information report receptors B, C, and D simultaneously receive the following reports (described in table 10, p. 111): financial and personnel status (R05) and sales analysis (R09).

3. C's decisional situation, *Personnel performance rating* (03), has been categorized as very structured and individual. All decision-making processes are possible and AUTOCRATIC-I is retained because only one information report receptor was involved. Table 10 (p. 111) shows that three reports are involved: Sales Statistics (R08), Personnel Presence (R04) and Statement of Accounts (R02).

4. D's decisional situation of *Sales performance* (05) is individual (one subordinate is involved) and the decision tree analysis (figure 14, p. 94, and table 6, p. 95) allows only one process: GROUP-1. In this case the two organizational positions involved, D and G, simultaneously receive the report entitled "Sales Statistics" (R07) previously noted in table 10 (p. 111).

The above reading of table 11 (p. 113) reflects the rationalization effort associated with the decisional situations of the simplified organization. The first humanization variable has enabled the identification of not only the organizational positions involved with each decisional situation but also the information report receptors.

## Psychological and Cognitive Types

The second humanization variable refers to MIS users, the decision makers, and to their psychological and cognitive types. Assume that the seven members of the organization have taken the Myers-Briggs test and that the systems designer has situated these individuals on the sensing-intuition and the thinking-feeling axes, and on the systematic, judicial, intuitive, and speculative classification (see table 8, p. 104). Also assume for example that the person occupying position A (see table 12, p. 114) is of the intuition-thinking (speculative) type. According to our research to date, A prefers a narrative report format, reading first and afterward receiving a verbal exposé. On the other hand, the person holding position C (assuming a sensing-thinking, systematic type) prefers a tabular or graphical report format. C also prefers to read reports but does not require that a subordinate provide a verbal interpretation. By locating

## TABLE 11

## ANALYSIS OF DECISIONAL SITUATIONS, ESTABLISHMENT OF DECISION-MAKING PROCESSES, AND IDENTIFICATION OF INFORMATION REPORT RECEPTORS

FIRST HUMANIZATION VARIABLE: DECISION MAKING PROCESSES

| DECISIONAL SITUATION | | | DECISION-MAKING PROCESSES DECISION TREE (Figure 14 and table 6) | | | DECISION-MAKING PROCESS | | RECEPTORS OF INFORMATION REPORTS |
|---|---|---|---|---|---|---|---|---|
| DECISION NUMBER | ORGANIZATION POSITION* | SITUATION DESCRIPTION | ANSWERS TO THE EIGHT QUESTIONS ABCDEFGH | TERMINAL NODE | QUESTIONS SITUATION TYPE | AVAILABLE PROCESSE(S) (table 6) | PROCESS RETAINED | |
| 07 | A | -organizational development plan | YNNYNYYN | 17 | GROUP | GROUP-II | GROUP-II | A,B,C,D (simultaneously) |
| 06 | B | - personnel evaluation and assignment | YYNNNYYN | 4 | GROUP | all | CONSULTATIVE-I | B,C,D (simulataneously) |
| 03 | C | - personnel performance rating | YYYNYY-Y | 3 | INDIVIDUAL | all | AUTOCRATIC-I | C |
| 05 | D | - sales performance | YYYYYY-N | 7 | INDIVIDUAL | GROUP-I | GROUP-I | D,G (simultaneously) |

* Vroom, Yetton, and Jago's decision-making processes model does not apply to organizational positions E, F and G. These positions are subordinate positions to which no other subordinate positions report. E,F, and G are the only positions to receive, respectively, the inputs associated to them in Table 10. Therefore, the corresponding decisional situations 02, 01, and 04 are not considered here.

TABLE 12

SECOND HUMANIZATION
VARIABLE: PSYCHOLOGICAL
AND COGNITIVE TYPES

ANALYSIS OF DECISION MAKERS AND ESTABLISHMENT OF
INFORMATION REPORTS PREFERENTIAL PRESENTATION FORMATS AND COMMUNICATION MEANS

| POSITION | CLASSIFICATION OF PSYCHOLOGICAL AND COGNITIVE TYPE | | INFORMATION REPORT | |
|---|---|---|---|---|
| | ACCORDING TO JUNG | ACCORDING TO NUTT | PREFERENTIAL PRESENTATION FORMAT | PREFERENTIAL COMMUNICATION MEANS (according to table 8) |
| A | intuition–thinking | speculative | narrative | textual/verbal |
| B | sensing–feeling | judicial | graphical/tabular | verbal |
| C | sensing–thinking | systematic | tabular/graphical | textual |
| D | intuition–feeling | intuitive | narrative | verbal |
| E | sensing–feeling | judicial | graphical/tabular | verbal |
| F | intuition–feeling | intuitive | narrative | verbal |
| G | sensing–thinking | systematic | tabular/graphical | textual |

114

each decision maker by types we have explored, the designer can pinpoint the types of formats preferred by each report receptor. This humanization effect adds significantly to the effectiveness of the MIS.

## Inquiring Systems

The third humanization variable deals with the designer who, however objective, is not impervious to human system's design considerations. The major contribution of this variable can be summarized in one word: structurability. In effect, Leibnizian, Lockean, Kantian, Hegelian, and Singerian inquiring systems refer progressively to more and more difficult problems, or less and less structured decisional situations. Table 13, (p. 116) depicts the structurability of the present example's seven decisional situations. As mentioned, it is an assumption that upper organizational levels are faced with more difficult situations than lower organizational levels. The hypothesis associated with this third humanization variable is that Singerian and Hegelian designers are more at ease with unstructured decisional situations and that Leibnizian and Lockean designers are more at ease with structured decisional situations. Semi-structured decisional situations have been assigned to Kantian designers. The implications, as far as the example is concerned, are the following:

• The Singerian designer is assigned to the organizational development plan decision because a broad perspective of the problem is required.

• The Hegelian designer is assigned to the personnel evaluation and assignment decision because a dialectic and creative synthesis is called for.

• The Kantian designer is assigned to the decision related to personnel performance, which in the present context is considered as being somewhat mechanical in nature because of the mix of data which must be identified and models or rules which must be established.

• The Kantian designer is also assigned to the decision on sales performance for essentially the same reason.

TABLE 13

THIRD HUMANIZATION
VARIABLE:
INQUIRING SYSTEMS

SYSTEMS DESIGNERS BY TYPE AND ASSIGNMENT
OF DESIGN TASKS AS A FUNCTION OF DECISIONAL SITUATIONS

| DECISIONAL SITUATION | | ORGANIZATION | STRUCTURABILITY* | PREFERRED |
|---|---|---|---|---|
| NUMBER | DESCRIPTION | POSITION | | DESIGNER TYPE |
| 07 | organizational development plan | A | unstructured | Singerian |
| 06 | personel evaluation and assignment | B | unstructured | Hegelian |
| 03 | personnel performance | C | semi-structured | Kantian |
| 05 | sales performance | D | semi-structured | Kantian |
| 02 | daily processing of personnel data | E | structured | Lockean |
| 01 | daily processing of accounting data | F | structured | Lockean |
| 04 | daily processing of sales data | G | structured | Leibnizian |

* The decisional situation structurability of organizational positions A, B, C, and D have been noted in table 11 in answer to question "C" of the decision tree. Nevertheless, we indicate in this table that C and D's decisional situations are semi-structured. We also define, for the sake of completion, E, F, and G's decisional situations.

# TABLE 14

## THE MIS REPORTING SUBSYSTEM - INFORMATION REPORTS ESTABLISHED IN COMPLIANCE WITH MIS HUMANIZATION THEORY

| DECISIONAL SITUATION NUMBER | DESCRIPTION | PREFERENTIAL INQUIRING SYSTEMS | INFORMATION REPORTS (INPUTS) NUMBER | DESCRIPTION | A Format | A Means | B Format | B Means | C Format | C Means | D Format | D Means | E Format | E Means | F Format | F Means | G Format | G Means |
|---|---|---|---|---|---|---|---|---|---|---|---|---|---|---|---|---|---|---|
| 07 | organizational development plan | Singerian | R10 | organizational status | n | te/v | g/ta | v | ta/g | te | n | v | - | - | - | - | - | - |
| 07 | organizational development plan | Singerian | R06 | economic context by region | n | te/v | g/ta | v | ta/g | te | n | v | - | - | - | - | - | - |
| 06 | personnel evaluation and assignment | Hegelian | R05 | financial and personnel status | - | - | g/ta | v | ta/g | te | n | v | - | - | - | - | - | - |
| 06 | personnel evaluation and assignment | Hegelian | R09 | sales analysis | - | - | g/ta | v | ta/g | te | n | v | - | - | - | - | - | - |
| 03 | personnel performance | Kantian | R08 | sales statistics | - | - | - | - | ta/g | te | - | - | - | - | - | - | - | - |
| 03 | personnel performance | Kantian | R04 | personnel presence | - | - | - | - | ta/g | te | - | - | - | - | - | - | - | - |
| 03 | personnel performance | Kantian | R02 | statement of accounts | - | - | - | - | ta/g | te | - | - | - | - | - | - | - | - |
| 05 | sales performance | Kantian | R07 | sales statistics | - | - | - | - | - | - | n | v | g/ta | v | - | - | ta/g | te |
| 02 | daily operational processing of personnel data | Lockean | R03 | employee description card | - | - | - | - | - | - | - | - | g/ta | v | - | - | - | - |
| 02 | daily operational processing of personnel data | Lockean | R02 | employee time card | - | - | - | - | - | - | - | - | g/ta | v | - | - | - | - |
| 01 | daily operational processing of accounting data | Lockean | R01 | sales register | - | - | - | - | - | - | - | - | - | - | n | v | - | - |
| 01 | daily operational processing of accounting data | Lockean | F01 | invoice/check | - | - | - | - | - | - | - | - | - | - | n | v | - | - |
| 04 | daily operational processing of sales data | Leibnizian | F03 | sales list | - | - | - | - | - | - | - | - | - | - | - | - | ta/g | te |

* Legend: g/ta=graphical/tabular; n=narrative; te=textual; ta/g=tabular/graphical; te/v=textual/verbal; v=verbal

** A dash (-) indicates that the organizational position is not involved with the information report nor with the corresponding decisional situation.

117

• The Lockean designer is assigned to two operational subsystems: personnel and accounting because data must initially be considered. The accounting model is already well known and established, therefore, there is no new model to invent; the personnel subsystem is essentially oriented toward identifying and gathering data because other decisional situations such as numbers 03 and 06 will make use of it.

• Finally, the Leibnizian designer is assigned the task of building the sales operational subsystem because, although data types are few in number and relatively simple, a relatively complex model must be elaborated.

Even though inquiring systems are presented as the third humanization variable it is one of the first to emerge. The design and development of an organizational information system corresponds to the project's management financial resoures and, most importantly, the personnel who are members of the systems design team. Consequently, their talents, their diverse analysis, and design capabilities must be used efficiently. Knowledge of each team member's favored inquiring system is essential.

# CONCLUSION

The three major MIS humanization variables have been applied to a fictititous example of a simplified organization. These variables are: Decision-making processes, user psychological and cognitive types, and designer inquiring systems. Although the organization has been qualified as simple and the example as fictitious, the use of these three design tools in the real world is quite direct.

The ability to summarize this design in only one table is a source of inspiration and encouragement. Table 14 (p. 117) acts as a synthesis of all that applies to the example. Everything that has been put forward on a conceptual basis and applied to the example is present.

How must one go about considering the human within the system when his or her organization is involved? How to assure the presence of the three humanization variables in one's design? The set of tables presented in this section can serve as a guide. A table similar to the last will help achieve a visible human oriented design.

# CHAPTER 4

# Phase IV - MIS Development, Exploitation, and Management

Organizing MIS development is the fourth phase of the MIS procedure. Many authors deal specifically with this phase. Auerbach Publisher's *Systems Development Management* series of portfolios is an excellent example of what has been and what will be written on the ever-evolving subject of MIS development.

This discussion of PHASE IV will be very brief. Figure 16 (p. 121) is a summary of the MIS development cycle (Rogers 1974). PHASE IV is an overlapping phase which covers all stages of the MIS procedure. Therefore, subjects discussed under the heading "MIS plan", such as participation, feasibility study, steering and user committees, and so forth, still apply. For the sake of completeness, two development items are worth mentioning: first, meetings and progress reports and, second, development times and costs.

The discussion of meetings and progress reports is almost a symbolic gesture! Human communication is *the* vital element in MIS development, hence, the need for frequent formal and informal meetings, whether to inform and engage user participation or to train, manage and motivate members of the design and development staff. User involvement in all phases of the MIS procedure is essential. The prevailing atmosphere during meetings must be one of participation, in which opinions, criticisms, commentaries and suggestions are openly and freely expressed. Such meetings should consist of a mix of presentations and discussions.[35]

Progress reports are also an essential part of the MIS procedure. They must be considered as elements which add to and complete the system's basic documentation. A progress report must be short, clear and concise, refer to the work accomplied, expose preliminary results, and present an update on project progress. Its main should be to keep top management informed on the evolving MIS procedure.

A general algorithm to predict and establish MIS development times and costs does not exist. Organizations differ from one to the other; therefore, results of time and cost studies done elsewhere must be approched with caution and adapted to reflect the peculiarities of one's own organization.

The cost/benefit analysis presents another considerable difficulty: how to quantify beforehand the benefits resulting from a yet-to-be-designed system. The problem is real for a good number of MIS benefits are of an intangible nature (for example, improved decision-making and staff attitudes). The organization's MIS design team - the manager-analyst team - must discover particular ways of justifying development costs, otherwise top management cannot be expected to give its consent to the allocation of resources for MIS development. The information in this book can add to this justification process.

# EXPLOITING AND MANAGING THE MIS

An organization must not only design and develop its MIS, it must run it! The degree of exploitation of an MIS depends upon its management and, more precisely, the management of the information resource which, in turn, depends upon control and change.

Once again, much has been written on the combined topics of MIS exploitation and management. I will neither repeat nor summarize all available material. Instead, I will address two pertinent topics: First, the information manager and, second, information system performance.

The information manager is a relatively recent organizational position. Its creation is the direct result of the real world shift from simple data processing toward the more complex and comprehensive information management. Information is now considered an organizational resource in much the same manner as finances, personnel, and inventory. Horton (1979) presented, in "Occupational Standard for the Information Resource Manager," a general description of the information manager's work: The manager directs the organization's overall information management program, which encompasses the coordination and synthesis of many disparate functional activities: libraries, information centers, computer centers, automatic data processing, word-processing centers, microform programs, printing, publishing, copying, reproduction, paperwork simplification and reduction programs, reports and forms control, and management, scientific and technical information systems. Horton's article is most complete. It describes both the general and specialized experience requirements, the quality of experience, special technical proficiency requirements, and candidate's evaluation. In short, the portrait of the information manager is most revealing.

Figure 16

MIS Development Cycle

| I MIS PROJECT SELECTION | II MIS SYSTEM PLAN | III MIS DESIGN | IV MIS IMPLEMENTATION | V MIS EVALUATION AND MODIFICATION | VI MIS EXPLOITATION | VII MIS MAINTENANCE AND UPDATING |
|---|---|---|---|---|---|---|
| PROBLEM DEFINITION AND EVALUATION | PRELIMINARY STUDY PLAN | SYSTEM DESIGN USING GLOBAL CONCEPTUAL FRAMEWORK | SYSTEM INSTALLATION NEW SYSTEM TEST | ACCEPTANCE EVALUATION OF NEW SYSTEM | SYSTEM OPERATION | SYSTEM ROUTINE MAINTENANCE AND CONTINUAL UPDATING |
| SOLUTION FEASIBILITY PROJECT EXTENT | PELIMINARY STUDY | MODULE (PROGRAMS AND PROCEDURES) ELABORATION | PARALLEL OPERATIONS WITH OLD SYSTEM AND NEW SYSTEM | COMPLETION OF COST-BENEFIT ANALYSIS STUDY | | |
| MIS FAMILIARIZATION SESSIONS | GENERAL PRE-DESIGN USING GLOBAL CONCEPTUAL FRAMEWORK | MODULES TESTING | | | | |
| | PROJECT CONTROL | | | | | |

Milestones (between phases): PROJECT COMMIT · SYSTEM COMMIT · SYSTEM TESTING · OLD TO NEW TRANSITION · POST INSTALLATION REVIEW · ONWARD UNTIL "THE END"

121

The topic of information system performance can be characterized in one word - *change*. What a discouraging yet challenging word!
Change must be warranted. Change for the sake of change is to be
avoided! Hence, the need for MIS control procedures and for gauging
its performance. Control implies procedural mechanisms for following
MIS exploitation (volume, costs, usage, etc.). In a certain way, control
is the precursor of performance, and performance is the precursor of
change. The word *performance* must be clearly understood if change is
to be significant and useful. What is understood by system performance?

Two words clarify the meaning of performance: *Efficacy* and
*efficiency*. Although these two words are often used interchangeably,
these definitions are distinct from one another (Longpré 1982):

1. Efficacy is the ratio — Input: processing. Efficacy refers to the
processing of data. An effective system produces the desired effect.
Input data are gauged by physical mechanisms such as volume,
quantity, resources. The quantity of data is related to the system's
processing potential. Therefore, constraints may result from either
data quantity available or processed. The quantity available is linked
to production, entry, classification, and storage mechanisms. The
quantity processed is proportional to the human resources available,
their flexibility and versatility to the transformation processes (computer programs, operational procedures), and to the types of information (output) required. Transformation processes are limited to
the operational resources available. Therefore, efficacy is defined as
being proportional to the quantity of data available for processing
and inversely proportional to the quantity of data effectively processed. Efficacy does not consider MIS users! If the mathematical
measure of efficacy is given by the ratio input: processing, the value
"1" suggests a perfectly effective system. In other words, if the value
of inputted data is greater than the value of processed data, an
accumulation of unused data will occur. Conversely, if the value of
inputted data is less than the value of processed data, the misuse of
operational resources is suggested.

2. Efficiency is the ratio — Output: input. Efficiency measures
the extent to which the desired effect has been reached. Efficiency
directly considers MIS users by referring to the accumulation of
information reports (output). The ratio, output: input, must be equal
or greater than "1" for efficiency to occur. If the value of output
information is less than the value of input data, the system will not
be efficient; a portion of available data is not being exploited. On the

other hand, if the value of output information is equal or greater than the value of input data, efficiency will be directly proportional to the mathematically obtained ratio.[36]

As I have argued, performance is a measure of change. The use of efficacy and efficiency to establish MIS performance and attempt to predict change is thereby possible. However, it is imperative to distinguish between the two measures: An MIS can be effective, but inefficient or vice versa. The changes to be made on an effective but inefficient system are not necessarily of the same kind that have to be made on an ineffective but efficient system.

# SUMMARIZING QUESTIONS

Bandyopadhyay (1977) presented a number of criteria for evaluating MIS conceptual design frameworks. His questions have been reformulated as follows:

1. Does the framework permit the elaboration of concepts and definitions in a global context which links information to decision?

2. Does it offer an insight and a useful guide to the supplying of information for better decision-making?

3. Does it deal with information needs at various hierarchical levels, for various hierarchical decision makers?

4. Do the framework concepts and ideas help resolve decisional situations related to operations, operational control, management control and stragetic planning?

5. Does the framework specifically address the definition and gauging of informational attributes - such as precision, pertinence, value - and does it relate them to various decisional attributes - such as importance, complexity, and critical state?

6. Does it explicitly recognize information cost?

7. Does it explicitly recognize that a better supply of information results in an increased value of decision-making processes?

8. Is it sufficiently flexible to be extended to complex situations reduced to simple situations?

9. Can it be understood and used by managers and analysts alike?

10. Once information needs have been defined, can it be used for project development and management purposes?

11. Does it illustrate that management models are an integral part of MIS and are not to be implemented in isolation?

12. Does it emphatically consider that a thorough analysis of information needs constitutes the very design basis of an MIS and that both the framework and the MIS must be oriented by a logical structure of the potential system?

How does the global conceptual framework rate? How many YES answers? How many NO answers? One thing is certain: The global framework will never be *complete*. In other words, it will always be possible and desirable to add other design considerations and to further refine its use. Why not consider the design of individual MIS's - made to measure - where every member of an organization is considered and the MIS humanization ideas are inserted in Computer Assisted Design (CAD) systems? There is no end in sight!

In conclusion, the documentation, analysis, and design form (figure 10, p. 74) and its three adjunct forms of the forms appendix: the decision analysis form (form-1, p. 151), the decision maker analysis form (form-2 p. 152) and the designer identification form (form-3 p. 153) constitute practical MIS design tools. Their usefulness rests in their capacity to answer the questions: Why? Who? How? How much? How many? When? Where? The ideas and concepts exposed in these pages will be useful to managers and analysts who are or who may eventually be members of MIS design teams. Perhaps they will remember that *Management Information Systems'* humanization is the topic of a future that is now!

# Creativity and Third Wave Tests

## Creativity Test

*How Creative Are You?*

The following test was designed by Eugene Randsepp of Princeton Creative Research, Inc. after studying characteristics of highly creative people. This test was presented in an article by Howard Nyles entitled "Business Probes the Creative Spark", which appeared in *Dun's Review* (January, 1980). Reprinted with the special permission of Dunn's Review, Copyright 1980, Dun and Bradstreet Publications Corporation.

To take the test
- Indicate after each statement whether you:
  - agree                         -  (A)
  - are in-between or
    do not know          -  (B)
  - disagree                   -  (C)
- Answer as accurately and frankly as possible.
- *Try* not to guess how a *creative* person might respond.
- There is no time limit.
- Circle the letter corresponding to your answer.
- The answers to this test and their respective values will be found at the end of this section. So will the test results!

1. I feel that a logical step-by-step method is best for solving problems.

   A (B) C

2. It would be a waste of time for me to ask questions if I had no hope of obtaining answers.

   (A) B C

3. I always work with a great deal of certainty that I am following the correct procedures for solving a particular problem.

   A (B) C

4. I concentrate harder on whatever interests me than do most people.

   (A) B C

5. When trying to solve a problem, I spend a lot of time analyzing it.

   (A) B C

6. I occasionally voice opinions in groups that seem to turn some people off.

   (A) B C

7. I spend a great deal of time thinking about what others think of me.

   (A) B C

8. Complex problems and situations appeal to me because I find them challenging.

   (A) B C

9. It is more important for me to do what I believe to be right than to try to win the approval of others.

   A (B) C

10. People who seem unsure and uncertain about things lose my respect.

    A B (C)

11. More than other people, I need to have things interesting and exciting.

    (A) B C

12. On occasion I get overly enthusiastic over things.

    (A) B C

13. I often get my best ideas when doing nothing in particular.

    A (B) C

14. I rely on intuitive hunches and the feeling of "rightness" or "wrongness" when moving toward the solution of a problem.

    (A) B C

126

15. I sometimes get a kick out of breaking the rules and doing things I'm not supposed to do.
     (A) B C

16. I like hobbies that involve collecting things.
     A B (C)

17. I feel I have capacities that have not been tapped as yet.
     (A) B C

18. Daydreaming has provided the impetus for many important projects.
     (A) B C

19. I like people who are objective and rational.
     (A) B C

20. I see myself as more enthusiastic and energetic than most people I know.
     A (B) C

21. I can get along more easily with people if they belong to about the same social and business class as myself.
     (A) B C

22. I have a high degree of aesthetic sensitivity.
     A (B) C

23. I have a highly developed capacity for self-instruction.
     (A) B C

24. I like people who are most sure of their conclusions.
     A (B) C

25. Inspiration has nothing to do with the successful solution of problems.
     A B (C)

26. When I'm engaged in an argument, the greatest pleasure for me would be for the person who disagrees with me to become a friend, even at the price of sacrificing my point of view.
     (A) B C

27. I tend to avoid situations in which I might feel inferior.
     (A) B C

28. In evaluating information, the source of it is more important to me than the content.
     (A) B C

29. I resent things being uncertain and unpredictable.
     (A) B C

30. I like people who follow the rule "business before pleasure".

    A   B   (C)

31. One's own self-respect is more important than the respect of others.

    A   (B)   C

32. I feel that people who strive for perfection are unwise.

    A   B   (C)

33. I prefer to work with others in a team effort rather than solo.

    (A)   B   C

34. I believe that creativity is restricted to specialized fields of endeavour.

    A   B   (C)

35. It is important for me to have a place for everything and everything in its place.

    A   (B)   C

36. Sometimes I am sure that other people can read my thoughts.

    (A)   B   C

37. The trouble with many people is that they take things too seriously.

    A   B   (C)

38. I have a great deal of initiative and self-starting ability.

    (A)   B   C

39. I have retained my sense of wonder and spirit of play.

    A   (B)   C

40. I can maintain my motivation and enthusiasm for my projects, even in the face of discouragement, obstacles or opposition.

    A   B   (C)

41. People who are willing to entertain "crackpot" ideas are impractical.

    A   B   (C)

42. I am more interested in what could be than what is.

    (A)   B   C

43. Even after I have made up my mind, I often can change it.

    (A)   B   C

44. I enjoy fooling around with new ideas, even if there is no practical payoff.     (A) B C

45. I think the statement: "Ideas are a dime a dozen", hits the nail on the head.     A (B) C

46. I do not like to ask questions that show ignorance.     (A) B C

47. Once I undertake a project, I am determined to finish it, even under conditions of frustration.     A (B) C

48. I sometimes feel that ideas come to me as if from some external source and that I am not directly responsible for them.     A B (C)

49. There have been times when I experienced an "avalanche" of ideas.     A (B) C

50. I try to look for ways of converting necessities to advantages.     A (B) C

51. It is wise not to expect too much of others.     A (B) C

52. I am able to more easily change my interests to pursue a job or career than I can change a job to pursue my interests.     (A) B C

53. Many creative breakthroughs are the result of change factors.     A (B) C

54. People who are theoretically oriented are less important than are those who are practical.     A (B) C

55. I feel it is important to understand the motives of people with whom I have to deal.     (A) B C

56. I can see things in terms of their potential.     A (B) C

57. When brainstorming in a group, I am able to think up more ideas more rapidly than can most others in the group.     A (B) C

58. I am not ashamed to express "feminine" interest (if man), or "masculine" interests (if woman), if so inclined.

    A (B) C

59. I tend to rely more on my first impressions and feelings when making judgments than on a careful analysis of the situation.

    A (B) C

60. I can frequently anticipate the solution to my problems.

    A (B) C

61. I often laugh at myself for my quirks and peculiarities.

    A B (C)

62. Only fuzzy thinkers resort to metaphors and analogies.

    A B (C)

63. When someone tries to get ahead of me in a line of people, I usually point it out to him.

    (A) B C

64. Problems that do not have clear-cut and un-ambiguous answers have very little interest for me.

    (A) B C

65. I usually work things out for myself rather than get someone to show me.

    (A) B C

66. I trust my feelings to guide me through experiences.

    (A) B C

67. I frequently begin work on a problem that I can only dimly sense and not yet express.

    (A) B C

68. I frequently tend to forget things such as names of people, streets, highways, small towns, etc.

    A B (C)

69. I have more capacity to tolerate frustration than does the average person.

    (A) B C

70. During my adolescence, I frequently had a desire to be alone and to pursue my own interests and thoughts.

    A B (C)

71. I feel that the adage: "Do unto others . . ." is more important than: "To thine own self be true."  A (B) C

72. Things that are obvious to others are not so obvious to me.  A B (C)

73. I feel that I may have a special contribution to give to the world.  (A) B C

74. I find that I have more problems than I can tackle, more work than there is time for.  A (B) C

75. Below is a list of adjectives and terms that describe people. Indicate with a check mark *ten* (10) words that best characterize you.

| | | |
|---|---|---|
| energetic | quick | alert |
| persuasive | efficient | curious |
| observant | helpful | organized |
| fashionable | perceptive | unemotional |
| self-confident | courageous | clear-thinking |
| persevering | stern | understanding |
| forward-looking ✗ | thorough | dynamic |
| cautious ✓ | ✓impulsive | self-demanding |
| habit-bound | determined | polished |
| resourceful | factual | ✓ realistic |
| egotistical | open-minded | ✓ modest |
| independent | ✓tactful | involved |
| good-natured ✓ | inhibited | absent-minded |
| predictable | enthusiastic | ✗ flexible |
| formal | innovative | ✓ sociable |
| informal | poised | well-liked |
| dedicated | acquisitive | restless |
| original | ✓ practical | retiring |

## Third Wave Test
*Are You of the Third Wave?*

The following test was inspired by the contents of Alvin Toffler's *The Third Wave*. It was designed after studying the characteristics of an absolutely phenomenal number of highly "third wave" people.

To take the test
- Indicate after each statement whether you:
  - agree          - (A)
  - are in-between or
    do not know    - (B)
  - disagree       - (C)
- Answer as accurately and frankly as possible.
- Try not to guess how a *third wave* person might respond.
- There is no time limit.
- Circle the letter corresponding to your answer.
- The answers to this test and their respective values will be found at the end of this section. So will the test results!

1. I feel that the super-battle of tomorrow will be between those who attempt to maintain the industrial society and those who are ready to surpass it.      A   B   C

2. I try tenaciously to protect the basic institutions of our industrial society.      A   B   C

3. I believe that the boundaries between the second (industrial) wave and the third (future) wave are confused and hazy.      A   B   C

4. I think that the most urgent problems are those related to energy, war, poverty, and the rupture of family links.      A   B   C

5. I favor the matrix organization where temporary groups are integrated into a radically new formal structure opposed to centralized control and which operates on the basis of multiple commands.

A   B   C

6. I feel that the major axis of tomorrow will be the home.

A   B   C

7. I do not agree with the popularity of do-it-yourself movements.

A   B   C

8. It is not essential for me to have rapid access to a computer.

A   B   C

9. I believe that present political structures are more and more outmoded and incapable of dealing with the complexities of today's world.

A   B   C

10. I suspect that there are honest and sincere people belonging to all three waves.

A   B   C

11. As far as I am concerned, the necessary characteristics of third-wave leaders are not yet well defined.

A   B   C

12. I am of the opinion that an industrial civilization is no longer capable of dealing with present day problems.

A   B   C

13. In the office of tomorrow, I feel that more and more people will be involved with decision making.

A   B   C

14. I consider myself an apostle of traditional nationalism.

A   B   C

15. I am not in favor of a democracy of minorities.

A   B   C

16. I think that it is important to have a global vision to solve problems.

A   B   C

17. I estimate that many distinctive features of the third-wave civilization are similar to those of first-wave societies.  A  B  C

18. I have a computer or a terminal linked to a computer.  A  B  C

19. I am concerned that most of the jobs of the future will be part time.  A  B  C

20. I do not think that political parties give the impression of each being the deformed image of the other.  A  B  C

21. I believe that we will never find *the* true cause of the third wave.  A  B  C

22. I agree that in the office of tomorrow, secretaries will have access to paradirectorial tasks and be implicated in design work and decision-making.  A  B  C

23. I believe that the computer amplifies social memory and at the same time makes it more dynamic.  A  B  C

24. Personally, I resist all initiatives which can bring about a more equitable economic world order.  A  B  C

25. Occasionally, I feel that the fears expressed by ecologists are ridiculous.  A  B  C

26. I am not in favor of flexible timetables.  A  B  C

27. I am opposed to the demassification of teaching.  A  B  C

28. It is important for me to present obstructions to decentralization, regionalism, and diversity.  A  B  C

29. I concede that it is necessary to restructure the world economy and provide it with a more just and equitable base.  A  B  C

30. I do not think that a strong leadership - even totalitarism - has anything to do with efficiency.  A  B  C

31. I share the view that most of the proponents of the second wave (industrial) are those who pull the reins of power within today's society.  A  B  C

32. I do not agree that everyday I make a multitude of feverish decisions.  A  B  C

33. I do not foresee that the plant of tomorrow will produce demassified and often personalized goods.  A  B  C

34. I believe that the development strategies of tomorrow will not be forthcoming from Washington, Moscow, Paris, or Geneva, but from Africa, Asia and Latin America.  A  B  C

35. I foresee that in our institutions of the future, it will be more and more important to create the position of Information Manager.  A  B  C

36. Environmental problems are not my priority.  A  B  C

37. I do not think it important to divide bureau-cracies suffering from gigantism.  A  B  C

38. I am not ready to experiment with various forms of more direct democracies.  A  B  C

39. I do not share the opinion that professional economists are incapable of explaining and elucidating the manner in which economic mechanisms really work.  A  B  C

40. I estimate that a more integrated problem-solving approach is required.  A  B  C

41. To my mind, a number of things which may appear to be anarchist are not.  A  B  C

42. It seems impossible to me that a society decentralize economic activities, communications and a good many other crucial procedures without having eventually to decentralize decision-making.  A  B  C

43. To my mind, the requirement to create new political institutions suggests the need for new family, educational, and business institutions.  A  B  C

44. Personally, I am not ready to put up a fight for individualized as opposed to standardized teaching in schools.  A  B  C

45. I estimate that crucial decisions on which our very survival depends can be made in the present political framework.  A  B  C

46. I believe that traditional economic thinking, whether occidental or marxist, has lost all contact with a reality undergoing rapid transformation.  A  B  C

47. Personally, I do not favor a more centralized and renewable energy system.  A  B  C

48. I oppose minority movements in a very characteristic fashion.  A  B  C

49. I am in favor of transnationalism and the devolution of power.  A  B  C

50. I share the view that in the next decades, human intelligence, intuition, and imagination will continue to be infinitely more important than machines.  A  B  C

\*\*\*

Answers to creativity test

- To compute your score, add up the points assigned to each item.

For each question, the first value is for A (agree), the second is for B (in-between or do not know) and the third is for C (disagree).

| | | |
|---|---|---|
| 1. -1, 0, 2 | 26. -1, 0, 1 | 51. 1, 0, -1 |
| 2. 0, 1, 2 | 27. -1, 0, 1 | 52. -2, 1, 0 |
| 3. 0, 1, 2 | 28. -2, 1, 2 | 53. 2, 1, 0 |
| 4. 3, 0, -1 | 29. -1, 0, 1 | 54. -2, 1, 0 |
| 5. 2, 1, 0 | 30. -1, 0, 1 | 55. 2, 0, -1 |
| 6. 2, 1, 0 | 31. 2, 1, 0 | 56. 2, 0, -1 |
| 7. -1, 0, 2 | 32. -2, 1, 0 | 57. 2, 0, -1 |
| 8. 2, 1, 0 | 33. -1, 1, 2 | 58. 2, 1, 0 |
| 9. 2, 0, -1 | 34. -1, 0, 1 | 59. 1, 0, -1 |
| 10. -1, 0, 2 | 35. -1, 0, 1 | 60. 2, 1, 0 |
| 11. 2, 1, 0 | 36. -2, 0, 2 | 61. 2, 0, -1 |
| 12. 3, 0, -1 | 37. -1, 0, 1 | 62. -2, 0, 2 |
| 13. 2, 0, -1 | 38. 2, 0, -1 | 63. 2, 1, 0 |
| 14. 3, 1, 0 | 39. 2, 0, -1 | 64. -1, 0, 1 |
| 15. 2, 1, 0 | 40. 2, 0, -1 | 65. 1, 0, -1 |
| 16. -1, 0, 1 | 41. -1, 0, 1 | 66. 2, 1, 0 |
| 17. 2, 1, 0 | 42. 2, 1, 0 | 67. 2, 1, 0 |
| 18. 3, 0, -1 | 43. 2, 1, 0 | 68. 2, 0, -1 |
| 19. -1, 0, 1 | 44. 2, 1, 0 | 69. 2, 1, 0 |
| 20. 2, 1, 0 | 45. -2, 0, 1 | 70. 2, 0, -1 |
| 21. -1, 0, 1 | 46. -1, 0, 1 | 71. -1, 0, 1 |
| 22. 3, 1, 0 | 47. 2, 0, -1 | 72. 2, 1, 0 |
| 23. 2, 1, 0 | 48. 2, 0, -1 | 73. 1, 0, -1 |
| 24. -1, 0, 1 | 49. 2, 1, 0 | 74. 2, 1, 0 |
| 25. -2, 0, 2 | 50. 2, 0, -1 | |

75. The following have values of 2: energetic, observant, persevering, resourceful, independent, dedicated, original, perceptive, courageous, enthusiastic, innovative, curious, dynamic, self-demanding, involved, flexible.

The following have values of 1: self-confident, forward-looking, informal, thorough, open-minded, alert, restless, determined.

The rest have values of 0.

Scoring     125-150     EXCEPTIONALLY CREATIVE
             90-124       VERY CREATIVE
             55-89        ABOVE AVERAGE
             35-54        AVERAGE
             15-34        BELOW AVERAGE
             -56-14       NONCREATIVE

Answers to third wave test

- To compute your score, add up the points assigned to each item.

- For each question, the first value is for A (agree), the second is for B (in-between or do not know) and the third is for C (disagree).

| | | |
|---|---|---|
| 1.  1, -1, -1 | 18.  3, 0, 0 | 35.  1, 0, -1 |
| 2.  -2, -1, 2 | 19.  -1, 0, 1 | 36.  -1, 0, 2 |
| 3.  1, 1, 1 | 20.  -1, 0, 1 | 37.  -1, 0, -1 |
| 4.  2, -1, -2 | 21.  1, -1, 1 | 38.  -1, 0, 1 |
| 5.  2, 0, -1 | 22.  3, 0, -3 | 39.  -1, 0, 1 |
| 6.  3, 0, -1 | 23.  2, 0, -3 | 40.  2, -1, -2 |
| 7.  -1, 0, 1 | 24.  -1, 0, 1 | 41.  2, 0, -3 |
| 8.  -1, 0, 1 | 25.  -1, 0, 1 | 42.  3, -1, -3 |
| 9.  1, 0, -1 | 26.  -1, 0, 1 | 43.  2, 0, -2 |
| 10.  1, 1, 1 | 27.  -1, 0, 1 | 44.  -1, 0, 2 |
| 11.  2, 1, 1 | 28.  -2, 0, 0 | 45.  -2, 0, 2 |
| 12.  1, 0, -1 | 29.  1, 0, -1 | 46.  1, 0, -1 |
| 13.  2, 0, -2 | 30.  1, -1, -1 | 47.  -1, 0, 1 |
| 14.  -3, 0, 1 | 31.  1, 1, 1 | 48.  -2, 0, 1 |
| 15.  -1, 0, 1 | 32.  -1, -1, 2 | 49.  1, 0, -1 |
| 16.  2, 0, -2 | 33.  -1, 0, 2 | 50.  5, 2, -4 |
| 17.  1, 0, 1 | 34.  1, 0, -1 | |

Scoring     61-75      GRAND MASTER OF THE THIRD WAVE
             46-60       COMMANDER OF THE THIRD WAVE
             31-45       OFFICER OF THE THIRD WAVE
             16-30       MEMBER OF THE THIRD WAVE
              1-15       MEMBER OF THE SECOND WAVE
            -62-0       MEMBER OF THE FIRST WAVE

Well, are you creative? Are you of the third wave? If your answer to both of these questions is yes, definitely carry on to Part II. If your answer to only one of these questions is yes, carry on to Part II. If your answer to both questions is no - carry on anyway -chances are you will become creative and "third wave"!

APPENDIX B

# MIS Structurability

## DATA-TRANSFORMATION

• Structured data can be submitted to all transformation types (structured, semi-structured, unstructured).

• Semistructured data can be submitted only to semi- and unstructured transformations.

• Unstructured data can be submitted only to unstructured transformations.

## TRANSFORMATION-INFORMATION

• A structured transformation can produce all information types (structured, semi-structured, unstructured).

• A semi-structured transformation can produce only semi-and unstructured information.

• An unstructured transformation can produce only unstructured information.

## INFORMATION-DECISION

• Structured information can be used for all decision types (structured, semi-structured, unstructured).

• Semi-structured information can be used for only semi- and unstructured decisions.

• Unstructured information can be used only for unstructured decisions.

# TABLE B-1

## FUNCTIONAL DEFINITIONS OF STUCTURED, SEMI-STRUCTURED, AND UNSTRUCTURED

ELEMENTS OF MIS SEQUENCE

| LEVEL OF STRUCTURABILITY | DECISION | INFORMATION (REPORT) | DATA | ACTION | TRANSFOR-MATION |
|---|---|---|---|---|---|
| STRUCTURED | can be made by computer | can be stored, identified and selectively retrieved from computer memory | can be stored, identified and selectively retrieved from computer memory | can be carried out by computer | can be effected by computer program |
| SEMI-STRUCTURED | can be made by computer or manually (or both) | | | | |
| UNSTRUCTURED | can only be made by human being | storage, identification and retrieval difficulties when stored in computer memory | storage, identification and retrieval difficulties when stored in computer memory | can only be carried out by human being | can be affected only by human being |

## DECISION-ACTION

- A decision can give rise to all action types (structured, semi-structured, unstructured). Action structurability is independent of the structurability of the decision which preceeded it.

This hypothesis is extremely useful in practice if for no other reason than its ability to structure manager-analyst team thinking whenever a MIS sequence is designed.

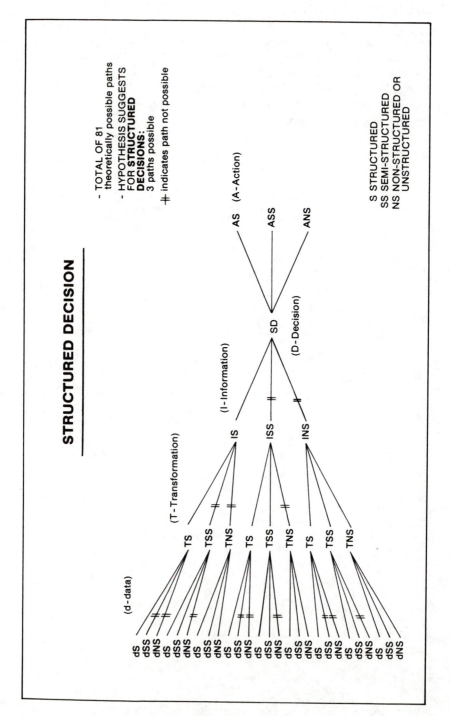

# STRUCTURED DECISION

- TOTAL OF 81 theoretically possible paths
- HYPOTHESIS SUGGESTS FOR **STRUCTURED DECISIONS:** 3 paths possible
- ≠ indicates path not possible

S STRUCTURED
SS SEMI-STRUCTURED
NS NON-STRUCTURED OR UNSTRUCTURED

(T - Transformation)
(I - Information)
(A - Action)
(D - Decision)
(d - data)

142

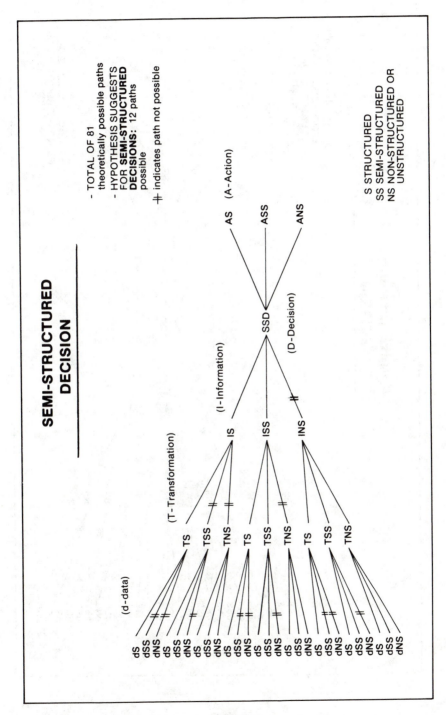

SEMI-STRUCTURED
DECISION

- TOTAL OF 81 theoretically possible paths
- HYPOTHESIS SUGGESTS FOR **SEMI-STRUCTURED DECISIONS**: 12 paths possible

⌗ indicates path not possible

(A-Action)

AS
ASS
ANS

SSD

(I-Information)          (D-Decision)

IS
ISS
INS

(T-Transformation)

TS
TSS
TNS
TS
TSS
TNS
TS
TSS
TNS

(d-data)

dS dSS dNS dS dSS dNS dS dSS dNS dS dSS dNS dS dSS dNS dS dSS dNS dS dSS dNS dS dSS dNS dS dSS dNS

S   STRUCTURED
SS  SEMI-STRUCTURED
NS  NON-STRUCTURED OR UNSTRUCTURED

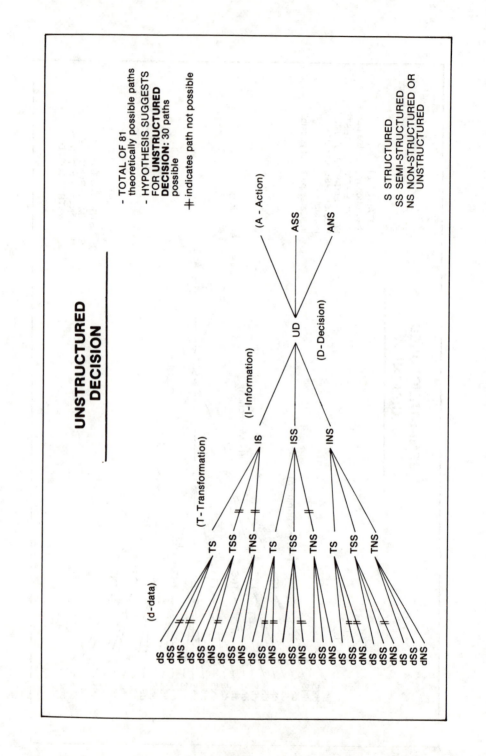

# UNSTRUCTURED DECISION

- TOTAL OF 81 theoretically possible paths
- HYPOTHESIS SUGGESTS FOR **UNSTRUCTURED DECISION**: 30 paths possible

╫ indicates path not possible

(A - Action)

ASS

ANS

UD

(D - Decision)

(I - Information)

IS

ISS

INS

(T - Transformation)

TS

TSS

TNS

TS

TSS

TNS

TS

TSS

TNS

(d - data)

dS
dSS
dNS
dS
dSS
dNS
dS
dSS
dNS
dS
dSS
dNS
dS
dSS
dNS
dS
dSS
dNS
dS
dSS
dNS
dS
dSS
dNS
dS
dSS
dNS

S    STRUCTURED
SS   SEMI-STRUCTURED
NS   NON-STRUCTURED OR UNSTRUCTURED

# Inquiring Systems Designer-Type Test

## A test

The following test is addressed to the systems designer whether he be a manager, an analyst, a computer expert, a student, a decision maker, etc. Least it be forgotten, we are all at one time or other involved in the design of some kind of system. The test appeared in the French weekly data processing magazine *01 Hebdo*. See: Hurtubise, R., translated title "System Designers, Who Are You?", *01 Hebdo*, no. 742, 28 March, 1983.

The test will help establish the designer type: leibnizian, lockean, kantian, hegelian, singerian.

To take the test

- Indicate after each statement whether you:
  - agree . . . answer      YES
  - disagree . . . answer    NO

- Answer as accurately and frankly as possible.

- Even if a statement may seem simple or even silly, please consider it! Think before answering!

- There is no time limit.

- The results will be found at the end of the test.

1. I can synthesize situations fairly easily.   YES   NO

2. I prefer unstructured problems.   YES   NO

3. At times, I begin a project by considering the relevant data; other times, I begin by establishing a model.   YES   NO

4. It is possible for me to synthesize ideas which may seem at the outset to be completely opposite.   YES   NO

5. I often find myself searching for more global or general views of a problem.   YES   NO

6. While searching for a solution, I find myself elaborating various models of possible solutions.   YES   NO

7. I prefer semi-structured problems.   YES   NO

8. Most of the time and in spite of empirical or personal considerations, I attempt to find a purely rational justification to a proposition or statement.   YES   NO

9. I prefer dealing with data rather than with models.   YES   NO

10. I am at ease during dialectical situations.   YES   NO

11. As far as I am concerned, it is impossible to separate data from models and conversely.   YES   NO

12. The precision of data preoccupies me.   YES   NO

13. Most of the time, I search for some combination of data and theoretical justifications.   YES   NO

14. I find it difficult to elaborate a model of a system without simultaneously knowing the pertinent data.   YES   NO

15. Most of the time, I reason by *induction*, that is, I proceed from a part to a whole, from particulars to generals.     YES  NO

16. I often ask myself if the assertions put forth are a good estimate of the true nature of things.     YES  NO

17. I enjoy "cost-benefit" type studies.     YES  NO

18. I am very interested in collecting statistical data.     YES  NO

19. Each time that I begin to study a new problem, I ask myself whether a sufficiently vast view of things has been taken.     YES  NO

20. I believe that truth is pragmatic.     YES  NO

21. For me, theory is what matters most.     YES  NO

22. When I undertake a study, I check to see if the correct questions have been asked.     YES  NO

23. I am very interested in operations research, queuing theory, inventory control, and computer simulation.     YES  NO

24. When solving a problem, I attempt to represent it by a rational model.     YES  NO

25. When solving a problem, I spend a certain amount of time finding out whether or not the proper objectives were addressed.     YES  NO

26. I prefer methods similar to brainstorming whereby a great number of ideas are generated as a result of interactions between a number of persons.     YES  NO

27. I prefer structured problems.     YES  NO

28. I dislike theorists.     YES  NO

29. I easily accept the states of conflict that result during a study.                                   YES  NO

30. My main objective consists in elaborating or illustrating a model which constitutes the very basis of a proposition or assertion.                                   YES  NO

31. Usually, I am not afraid to face ideas which differ significantly from existing assertions.                                   YES  NO

32. I recognize that I can easily work with persons who are neither objective nor rational.                                   YES  NO

33. I am forever on the lookout for statistics which support assertions, systems, etc.                                   YES  NO

34. I find it difficult during a project to edge away objectively from the system under study.                                   YES  NO

35. For me, truth is mainly analytical.                                   YES  NO

36. To my mind, most solutions reflect the unique personality of the persons involved.                                   YES  NO

37. I believe that one must first study data before attempting to justify a theory or model.                                   YES  NO

38. When attempting to solve a problem, I ask myself what is the probability that someone is correct.                                   YES  NO

39. When I solve a problem, I search for the "true" and the "false", the "yes" and the "no".                                   YES  NO

40. For me, truth is "synthetic", that is, it can be found in both theory and empiricism.                                   YES  NO

41. Most of the time, I reason by *deduction*, that is, I proceed from a whole to a part, from generals to particulars.                                   YES  NO

42. Often when an idea is put forth, I look for its contrary.                                   YES  NO

43. I believe it is important to have as many views as possible of a problem.  YES  NO

44. For me, truth is discovered following an agreement or a synthesis of two or more different models.  YES  NO

45. I consider valid all possible means to understand a problem.  YES  NO

46. To my ind, truth is discovered as a result of a state of conflict or debates existing between the supporters of an opinion on the one hand and the supporters of the contrary opinion on the other hand.  YES  NO

47. I attempt to justify an affirmation with objective data.  YES  NO

48. When solving a problem, I often rely on my intuition.  YES  NO

49. When study or analysis results are presented to me, I wish to know how they were arrived at.  YES  NO

50. I often look for alternatives or new options.  YES  NO

51. During a study, I like to observe and report my observations.  YES  NO

52. During a project, I prefer to proceed "step by step".  YES  NO

Answers to test

- In each of the five following columns, circle the question numbers for which you have given a YES answer.

- The column with the highest number of circled (YES) answers suggests the preferential inquiring system and, consequently, the analyst or designer type.

| 8 | 9 | 3 | 1 | 2 |
|---|---|---|---|---|
| 12 | 15 | 6 | 2 | 19 |
| 21 | 16 | 7 | 4 | 20 |
| 23 | 18 | 11 | 5 | 22 |
| 24 | 27 | 13 | 10 | 25 |
| 27 | 33 | 14 | 28 | 26 |
| 30 | 37 | 17 | 29 | 28 |
| 35 | 38 | 39 | 31 | 32 |
| 39 | 39 | 40 | 32 | 34 |
| 41 | 47 | 43 | 42 | 36 |
| 49 | 51 | 50 | 44 | 45 |
| 52 | 52 | 52 | 46 | 48 |

total
(maximum
values of
12 for each
column)  Liebnizian Lockean  Kantian  Hegelian Singerian

# APPENDIX D
# FORMS APPENDIX

FORM-1

## THE GLOBAL CONCEPTUAL DESIGN FRAMEWORK—
## THE DECISION ANALYSIS FORM

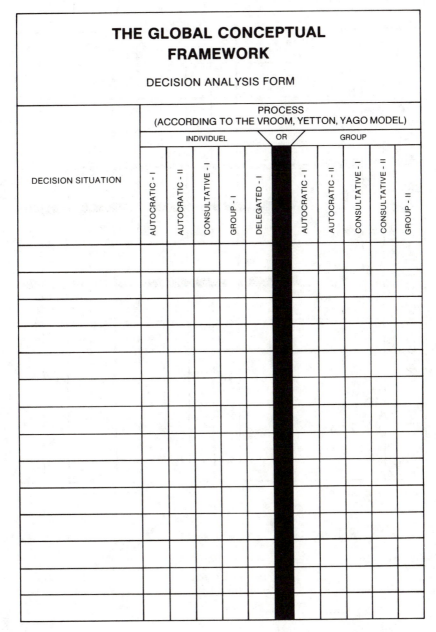

**THE GLOBAL CONCEPTUAL FRAMEWORK**

DECISION ANALYSIS FORM

| DECISION SITUATION | PROCESS (ACCORDING TO THE VROOM, YETTON, YAGO MODEL) | | | | | OR | | | | | |
|---|---|---|---|---|---|---|---|---|---|---|---|
| | INDIVIDUEL | | | | | | GROUP | | | | |
| | AUTOCRATIC - I | AUTOCRATIC - II | CONSULTATIVE - I | GROUP - I | DELEGATED - I | | AUTOCRATIC - I | AUTOCRATIC - II | CONSULTATIVE - I | CONSULTATIVE - II | GROUP - II |
| | | | | | | | | | | | |
| | | | | | | | | | | | |
| | | | | | | | | | | | |
| | | | | | | | | | | | |
| | | | | | | | | | | | |
| | | | | | | | | | | | |
| | | | | | | | | | | | |
| | | | | | | | | | | | |
| | | | | | | | | | | | |
| | | | | | | | | | | | |
| | | | | | | | | | | | |
| | | | | | | | | | | | |
| | | | | | | | | | | | |
| | | | | | | | | | | | |
| | | | | | | | | | | | |

FORM-2

# THE GLOBAL CONCEPTUAL FRAMEWORK—
## THE DECISION MAKER ANALYSIS FORM

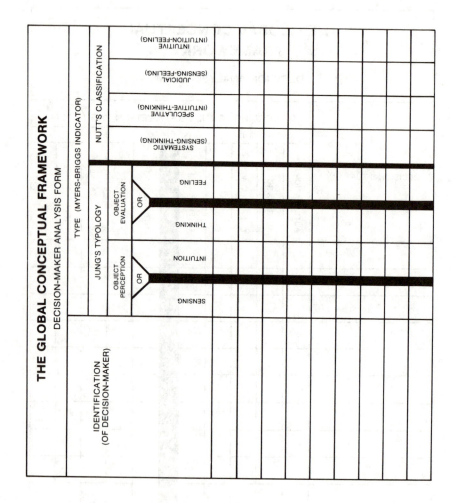

## THE GLOBAL CONCEPTUAL FRAMEWORK—
## THE DESIGNER IDENTIFICATION FORM

# THE GLOBAL CONCEPTUAL FRAMEWORK

THE DESIGNER IDENTIFICATION FORM

| IDENTIFICATION (OF DESIGNER) | PREFERENTIAL INQUIRING SYSTEM (C.W. CHURCHMAN'S CLASSIFICATION) | | | | | | | | | | | |
| --- | --- | --- | --- | --- | --- | --- | --- | --- | --- | --- | --- | --- |
| | LEIBNIZIAN | LOCKEAN | KANTIAN | HEGELIAN | SINGERIAN | | | | | | | |
| | | | | | | | | | | | | |
| | | | | | | | | | | | | |
| | | | | | | | | | | | | |
| | | | | | | | | | | | | |
| | | | | | | | | | | | | |

# NOTES

1    See two of Norbert Weiner's writings: *Cybernetics*, John Wiley and Sons, Inc., New York, 1948 and *The Human Use of Human Beings: Cybernetics and Society*, Doubleday, New York, 1950.

2    In view of this book's practical aspect, I will not differentiate between "systems theory," "general theory of systems," "theory of general systems," etc. I prefer to leave these highly intellectual matters to the theorists who, I am certain, will one day clarify the ambiguity which resulted from the title of L. von Bartalanffy's book: *General System Theory* (Braziller, New York, 1968). That is, does the adjective "general" qualify "system" or "theory"?

3    See: Samuelson, K., Borko, H., Amey, G.X., *Information Systems and Networks*, North-Holland Publishing Company, Amsterdam, 1977, page 7. It is a citation from C.W. Churchman's book: *The Systems Approach*, Dell Publishing Company, New York, 1968.

4    See: Fried, L., Objectives and Requirements of a Good Feasibility Study, *Systems Development Management*, Auerbach Publishers, Inc., portfolio no. 32-03-01, New Jersey, 1977 and Conducting the Feasibility Study, *Systems Development Management*, Auerbach Publishers, Inc., portfolio no. 32-03-02, New Jersey, 1976.

5    See: Malouin, J.-L., Landry, M., "La validation: activité critique pour une prise de décision éclairée" (Validation: A Critical Activity for Informed Decision Making), *CA Magazine*, September, 1979.

6    For a more complete description, please see: Sackman, H., *Delphi Critique*, Lexington Books, Massachusetts, 1975.

7    See also: Filiatreault, P., Perrault, Y.G., *L'administrateur et la' prise de décision* (Decision Making and the Administrator), Éditions du Jour, Montréal, 1974. By permission.

8    See: Samuelson, K., Bordo, H., Amey, G.X., *Information Systems and Networks*, North-Holland Publishing Company, Amsterdam, 1977.

9    A quantitative theory of information as exposed in: Shannon, C.E., Weaver, W., *The Mathematical Theory of Communications*, University of Illinois Press, Urbana, Illinois, 1949.

10   See also: Ricker, R.P., Data and Information, Are They Synonyms, *Journal of Systems Management*, September, 1979.

11   See: Kirkley, J.L., "Too Much to Read", *Datamation*, December, 1981: "Fighting the Paper Chase", *Time Magazine*, November, 23, 1981; Wilkinson, J.W., "Guidelines for Designing Systems", *Journal of Systems Management*, December, 1974.

12   On historical topics, see: *Management Information Systems and Organizational Behavior* by Pat-Anthony Federico, Kim E. Brun and Douglas B. McCalla (Praeger Publishers, New York, 1980) and "The MIS Challenge" by André Gingras (XXIII TIMS Symposium, Athens, Greece, 1977).

13   See also: Hunt, E., Makous, W., "Some Characteristics of Human Information Processing" in Ton, J.T., editor, *Advances in Information Systems Science* vol. 2, Plenum Press, New York, 1969, pages 283-335.

155

14 "Logical classification" and "documentation, analysis, and design form" will be described later in this book.

15 Perhaps the most complete source of references on the subject of Data Dictionary/Directory Systems can be found in numerous portfolios included in *Data Base Systems,* Auerbach Publishers Inc., New Jersey. The reader is directed to two references contained in *Data Base Systems.* Both are by Bernard K. Plagman: Data Dictionary/Directory System: A Tool for Data Administration and Control (portfolio no. 22-01-02); and Alternative Architectures for Active Data Dictionary/Directory Systems (portfolio no. 22-04-02). A comparative analysis of available data dictionary packages can be found in: Curtice, R.M., Dieckmann, E.M., A Survey of Data Dictionaries, *Datamation,* March, 1981.

16 Since the original "Industrial Dynamics" book, Jay W. Forrester has written a number of "dynamics books": *Urban Dynamics,* The M.I.T. Press, Massachusetts, 1969, *World Dynamics,* Wright-Allen Press, Massachusetts, 1971, and *Principles of Systems,* second edition, Wright-Allen Press, Massachusetts, 1968.

17 Lucas, H.C. 1976. *The Analysis, Design and Implementation of Information Systems.* New York: McGraw-Hill, page 27.

18 The global framework is not limited solely to the four tables and to the three links. An applications version of the global framework can represent all of the following organizational elements: mission, goal, objectives, programs (in the sense of program planning and budgeting systems (PPBS)), decisions, information, reporting processing, operational or administrative procedures, computer application programs, data, activity, action, task description, resources required or available (human, financial, material, etc.). Emphasis must remain, however, on the links or relations between the various tables.

19 The global framework is not rigidly confined to 4 columns and 3 rows. Rather its application to a particular organization consists in elaborating a set of tables where, theoretically, there are as many columns as there are levels within the organization and as many rows as there are levels of structurability.

20 Reproduced by permission.

21 The catalyst and the communication means columns is borrowed from the framework of R. Karni and S. Beraha. See: Karni, R., Beraha, S., A Definition and Design Framework for Management Information, *Information and Management,* no. 2, 1979.

22 See: Schewe, C.D., The Management Information System-User: An Exploratory Behavorial Analysis, *Academy of Management Journal,* vol. 19, no. 4, December, 1976; Lucas, H.C. Jr., User-Oriented Systems Analysis and Design, *Systems Development Management,* portfolio no. 33-02-03, Auerbach Publishers Inc., New Jersey, 1981; Moran, T.P., ed., The Psychology of Human - Computer Interaction, *ACM Computing Surveys,* special issue, vol. 13, no. 1, March, 1981; Yves, B., Hamilton, S., Davis, G.B., A Framework for Research in Computer-Based Management Information Systems, *Management Science,* vol. 26, no. 9, September, 1980.

23 See: Henderson, J.C., Nutt, P.C., The Influence of Decision Style on Decision Making Behaviour, *Management Science,* vol. 26, no. 4, April, 1980.

24 Portions of this section are reproduced by permission (*Decision Science*).

25  Jago and Vroom haved not maintained this dichotomy. We shall because the designer must identify the various information report users, and an analysis of organizational decisions as viewed from the decision-making hierarchy must consider whether one or many subordinates are affected. See: Jago, A.G., Vroom, V.H., An Evaluation of Two Alternatives to the Vroom/Yetton Normative Mode, *Academy of Management Journal*, vol. 23, no. 2, 1980.

26  Jago and Vroom do not refer to information sufficiency (H). For our present purposes, it is retained as an essential part of the model viewed from the organization's informational structure.

27  See three articles: Bariff, M.L., Lusk, E.J., Cognitive and Personality Tests for the Design of Management Information Systems, *Management Science*, vol. 23, no. 8, April, 1977; Vasarhelyi, M.A., *Cognitive Style Tailored Information Systems*, working paper no. 374A, Graduate School of Business, Columbia University, November, 1980; Alavi, M., Henderson, J.C., An Evolutionary Strategy for Implementing a Decision Support System, *Management Science*, vol. 27, no. 11, November, 1981.

28  See: Lake, D.G., Miles, M.B., Earle, R.B. Jr., *Measuring Human Behaviour*, Teachers College Press, Columbia University, New York, 1973.

29  The reader is referred to an article by E.J. Lusk and M. Kersnick, The Effect of Cognitive Style and Report Format on Task Performance: The MIS Design Consequences, *Management Science*, vol. 25, no. 8, August, 1979. See also two Ph. D. dissertations: Amador, J.A., *Information Formats and Decision Performance: An Experimental Investigation*, Ph.D. thesis, University of Florida, 1977; and Bybee, C.R., *Facilitating Decision-Making through Information Presentation Formats*, Ph.D. thesis, University of Wisconsin (Madison), 1978.

30  At the time of writing, the main reference to this incredible work is in French. See Lessoil B., Lafontaine, R., *L'univers des auditifs et des visuels* (The World of Auditives and Visuals), Editions du Nouveau Monde, Québec, 1981.

31  An interesting approach to MIS design was presented by Kaiser and Bostrom. They considered the MIS Project Team and identified them in terms of the Jungian typology as established by the Myers-Briggs indicator. Please see: Kaiser, K.M., Bostrom, R.P., Personality Characteristics of MIS Project Teams: An Empirical Study and Action-Research Design, *MIS Quarterly*, December, 1982.

32  Churchman, C. West, *The Design of Inquiring Systems: Basic Concepts of Systems and Organization*, Basic Books, New York, 1971. See also: Mitroff, I.I., Turoff, M., Philosophical and Methodological Foundations of Delphi in Linstone, H.A., Turoff, M., *The Delphi Method: Techniques and Applications*, Addison-Wesley, Massachusetts, 1975.

33  Vroom, Yetton and Jago's normative model applies to decisional situations where at least one subordinate is involved. Therefore, I have not considered the decisional situations (02, 01, and 04) belonging to organizational positions E, F, and G, which use as inputs employee time card (F02), invoice/check (F01), and sales list (F03).

34  Another designer could have selected another decision-making process. My goal consists not so much in justifying choices as in illustrating a method and procedure. I leave the reader with the pleasure of justifying my choices or choosing others.

35 Throughout this book, I have attempted to explicitly or implicitly refer to the topic of resistance to MIS. An interesting article which addressed *theories* of resistance to MIS and how knowledge of these theories can guide the implementation strategies and tactics chosen by MIS implementors is: Markus, M. Lynne, Power, Politics and MIS Implementation, *Communications of the ACM*, vol. 26, no. 6, June, 1983.

36 The assigning of values to *input, processing* and *output* can be done by the various users and analysts (a scale of 1 to 10 can be used). The fact that these values are subjective poses no concern. The fact that they be subjective is very significant. If each user and analyst attributes values to input, processing and output, the three resulting average values can be compared. In this manner, efficacy and efficiency can be established from relatively unstructured situations: narrative texts, verbal customer complaints, missed sales opportunities, etc.

# BIBLIOGRAPHY

Ackoff, R.L. 1971. "Towards a System of Systems Concepts". *Management Science*, vol. 17, no. 11, July

Alavi, M., and J.C. Henderson. 1981. "An Evolutionary Strategy for Implementing a Decision Support System". *Management Science*, vol. 27, no. 11, November.

Anthony, R.N. 1965. *Planning and Control Systems: A Framework for Analysis.* Boston: Division of Research, Graduate School of Business Administration, Harvard University.

Argyris, C. 1971. "Management Information Systems: The Challenge to Rationality and Emotionality". *Management Science*, vol. 17, no. 6, February.

Athey, T.H. 1977. "Fundamental Systems Concepts". *Journal of Systems Management*, November.

Bandyopadhyay, R. 1977. "Information for Organizational Decision Making - A Literature Review". *IEEE Transactions on Systems, Man, and Cybernetics*, vol. SMC-7, no. 1, January.

Bariff, M.L., and E.J. Lusk, 1977. "Cognitive and Personality Tests for the Design of Management Information Systems". *Management Science*, vol. 23, no. 8, April.

Bartalanffy, L. von. 1968. *General System Theory.* New York: Braziller.

Blumenthal, S.C. 1969. *Management Information Systems: A Framework for Planning and Development.* New Jersey: Prentice-Hall.

Briggs Myers, Isabel. 1962. *The Myers-Briggs Type Indicator - Manual (1962).* Palo Alto, California: Consulting Psychologists Press.

—. 1979. *Introduction to Type.* Second edition. Gainesville, Florida: Center for Applications of Psychological Type.

Carper, W.B., 1977. "Human Factors in MIS". *Journal of Systems Management,* November.

Churchman, C. West. 1968. *The Systems Approach.* New York: Dell Publishing Company.

—. 1971. *The Design of Inquiring Systems: Basic Concepts of Systems and Organization.* New York: Basic Books.

Curtuce, R.M., E.M. Dieckmann. 1981. "A Survey of Data Dictionaries". *Datamation,* March.

Dalkey, N., and O. Helmer. 1963. "An Experimental Application of the Delphi Method to the Use of Experts". *Management Science.* April, no. 3, vol. 9.

Dearden, J. 1965. "How To Organize Information Systems". *Harvard Business Review,* vol. 43, no. 2, March-April.

de Rosnay, J. 1975 and 1977. *Le macroscope, vers une vision globale* (The Macroscope, Towards a Global View). Paris: Editions du Seuil.

—. 1979. *Macroscope: A New World Scientific System.* New York: Harper and Row.

Elam, P.G. 1979. "User-Defined Information System Quality". *Journal of Systems Management,* August.

Eldin, H.K., and F.M. Croft. 1974. *Information Systems - a Management Science Approach.* New York: Petrocelli Books.

Filiatreault, P., and Y.G. Perrault. 1974. *L'administrateur et la prise de décision* (Decision Making and the Administrator). Montréal: Editions du Jour.

Forrester, J.W. 1961. *Industrial Dynamics.* Massachusetts: M.I.T. Press.

—. 1968. *Principles of Systems.* Second edition. Massachusetts: Wright-Allen Press.

—. 1969. *Urban Dynamics.* Massachusetts: M.I.T. Press.

—. 1971. *World Dynamics.* Massachusetts: Wright-Allen Press.

Fried, L. 1976. "Conducting the Feasibility Study". *Systems Development Management.* New Jersey: Auerbach Publishers, Inc., portfolio no. 32-03-02.

—. 1977. "Objectives and Requirements of a Good Feasibility Study". *Systems Development Management.* New Jersey: Auerbach Publishers, Inc., portfolio no. 32-03-01.

—. 1978. "Selecting and Using Consultant Services". *Systems Development Management.* New Jersey: Auerbach Publishers, Inc., portfolio no. 31-01-06.

Gaborro, J.J., and J.P. Kotter. 1980. "Managing your Boss". *Harvard Business Review,* January-February.

Galitz, W.O. 1980. *Human Factors in Office Automation.* Atlanta, Georgia: Life Office Management Association, Inc.

Gallagher, C.A. 1974. "Perceptions of the Value of a Management Information System". *Academy of Management Journal,* vol. 17, no. 1, March.

Gerrity, T.P. 1971. "Design of Man-Machine Decision Systems: An Application to Portfolio Management". *Sloan Management Review,* Winter.

Gorry, G.A., and M.S. Scott-Morton. 1971. "A Framework for Management Information Systems". *Sloan Management Review,* vol. 13, no. 1, Fall.

Henderson, J.C., P.C. Nutt. 1980. "The Influence of Decision Style on Decision Making Behaviour". *Management Science,* vol. 26, no. 4, April.

Holmes, R.W. 1970. "Twelve Areas to Investigate for Better MIS". *Financial Executive,* July.

Horton, F.W. 1979. "Occupational Standard for the Information Resource Manager". *Journal of Systems Management,* May.

Horton, F.W., and D.A. Marchand. 1982. *Information Management in Public Administration.* Arlington, Virginia: Information Resources Press.

Hurtubise, R 1970. "L'analyse de systèms bref aperçu sur une nouvelle discipline (Systems Analysis, Brief Overview of a New Discipline). *La Revue Commerce.* April.

—. 1976. *Informatique et information* (Data Processing and Information). Montréal and Paris: Agence d'ARC and Editions d'Organisation.

—. 1978. *La gestion de l'information* (The Management of Information). Montréal and Paris: Agence d'ARC and Editions d'Organisation.

—. 1980. *A la recherche du SIG* (In Search of the MIS). Montréal: Agence d'ARC.

—. 1980. "Êtes-vous un gestionnaire de troisiéme vague?" (Are You a Third Wave Manager?). *La Revue Commerce,* Octobre.

—. 1981. *L'administrateur québecois et les systèmes* (Systems and the Québec Administrator). Montréal: Agence d'ARC.

—. 1981. "Évaluer vos rapports d'information!" (Evaluate your Management Reports). *La Revue Commerce,* April.

—. 1981."Comment concevoir un système d'information"(How to Design a Management Information Systems). *La Revue Commerce,* November.

—. 1981. "L'humain dans la conception des systèmes d'information" (The Human in the Design of Information Systems). *Informatique et Gestion,* no. 129, December.

—. 1982. *L'humain dans le système* (The Human within the System): Montréal Agence d'ARC.

Jago, A.G., and V.H. Vroom. 1980. "An Evaluation of Two Alternatives to the Vroom/Yetton Normative Model". *Academy of Management Journal,* vol. 23, no. 2.

Kaiser, K.M., and R.P. Bostrom. 1982. "Personality Characteristics of MIS Project Teams: An Empirical Study and Action-Research Design". *MIS Quarterly,* December.

Karni, R., and S. Beraha. 1979. "A Definition and Design Framework for Management Information." *Information and Management,* no. 2.

# Bibliography

King, J.L., and E.L. Schrems. 1978. "Cost Benefit Analysis in Information Systems Development and Operation". *ACM Computing Surveys*, vol. 10, no. 1, March.

King, W.R. 1978. "Strategic Planning For Management Information Systems". *MIS Quarterly*, March.

Kolb, D.A., I.M. Rubin, and J.M. McIntyre. 1974. *Organizational Psychology - A Book of Readings*. (Second edition). New Jersey: Prentice Hall.

Lake, D.G., M.B. Miles, and R.B. Earle Jr. 1973. *Measuring Human Behaviour*. New York: Teachers College Press, Columbia University.

Landry, M., and J.-L. Malouin. 1976. "La complémentarité des approches systémique et scientifique dans le domaine des sciences humaines" (Complementarity of the Systems and Scientific Approaches in The Human Sciences). *Relations Industrielles*, vol. 31, no. 3.

Lasfargues, Y. 1976. *Une informatique par et pour les gestionnaires* (A Data Processing by and for Managers). Paris and Montréal: Editions d'Organisation, Institut francais de gestion and Agence d'ARC.

Lemoigne, J.L. 1977. *La théorie du système général-théorie de la modélisation (The Theory of the General System - Modeling Theory.)*. Paris: Presses Universitaries de France.

—. "La théorie du systéme d'information organisationnel" (The Theory of the Organizational Information System). *Informatique et Gestion*. no. 102, December.

Lessoil, B., R. Lafontaine. 1981. *L'univers des quditifs et des visuels* (The World of the Auditives and the Visuals). Québec: Editions du Nouveau Monde.

Longpré, L.-P. 1980. "Système d'information aux fins de gestion selon l'approche des communications" (Management Information Systems and the Communications Approach). *La Revue Commerce*, May.

Longpré, L.-P. 1982. "La différence entre efficience et efficacité" (The Difference between Efficacy and Efficiency). *La Revue Commerce*, January.

Lucas, H.C., K.W. Clowes, and R.B. Kaplan. 1974. "Frameworks for Information Systems". *Canadian Journal of Operational Research and Information Processing*, vol. 12, no. 3, October.

—. 1974. *Toward Creative Systems Design*. New York: Columbia University Press.

—. 1975. "Letters to the Editor, the Radford Framework". *Canadian Journal of Operational Research and Information Processing*. vol. 13, no. 1, February.

Lucas, H.C. Jr. 1981. "User - Oriented Systems Analysis and Design". *Systems Development Management*, New Jersey: Auerbach Publishers, Inc., portfolio no. 33-02-03.

Lusk, E.J., and M. Kersnick. 1979. "The Effect of Cognitive Style and Report Format on Task Performance: The MIS Design Consequences". *Management Science*, vol. 25, no. 8, August.

Malouin, J.-L., and M. Landry. 1979. "La validation: activité critique pour une prise de décision éclairée" (Validation: A Critical Activity for Informed Decision Making). *CA Magazine*, September.

Mason, R.O., and I.I. Mitroff. 1973. "A Program for Research on Management Information Systems". *Management Science*, vol. 19, no. 5, January.

Matthies, L., and Ellen Matthies. 1977. "Interviews". *World of Systems*, Colorado Springs: Management Research Society, no. 121.

Menkus, B. 1981. "Why Hasn't Word Processing Worked Better?". *Journal of Systems Management*, November.

Moder, Joseph, and Cecil R. Philips. 1970. *Project Management with CPM and PERT*, New York: Van Nostrand Reinhold Company. Second edition.

Moran, R.P. 1981. "The Psychology of Human - Computer Interaction". *ACM Computing Surveys*, vol. 13, no. 1, March.

Niles, H. 1980. "Business Probes the Creative Spark". *Dun's Review.* vol. 115, no. 1, January.

Nutt, P.C. 1979. "The Influence of Decision Styles on the Use of Decision Models". *Technological Forecasting and Social Change,* vol. 14, no. 1.

Olson, M.H., and H.C. Lucas Jr. 1982. "The Impact of Office Automation on the Organization: Some Implications for Research and Practice". *Communications of the ACM,* vol. 25, no. 11, November.

Optner, S.L. 1965. *Systems Analysis for Business and Industrial Problem Solving.* New Jersey: Prentice-Hall.

Osborn, Alex F. 1963. *Applied Imagination, Principles and Procedures of Creative Problem Solving.* Third edition (revised edition). New York: Charles Scribners Sons.

Plagman, B.K. "Data Dictionary/Directory System: A Tool for Data Administration and Control". *Data Base Systems.* New Jersey: Auerbach Publishers, Inc., portfolio no. 22-01-02.

—. "Alternative Architectures for Active Data Dictionary/Directory Systems". *Data Base Systems.* New Jersey: Auerbach Publishers, Inc., portfolio no. 22-04-02.

Radford, K.J. 1973. *Information Systems in Management.* Virginia: Reston Publishing Company.

Ricker, R.P. 1979. "Data and Information, Are They Synonyms", *Journal of Systems Management.* September.

Rogers, L.A. 1974. "In Plant Education Develops Better Systems Analysis". *Journal of Systems Management,* November.

Sackman, K., H. Bordo, and G.X. Amey. 1977. *Information Systems and Networks,* Amsterdam: North-Holland Publishing Company.

Schewe, C.D. 1976. "The Management Information System-User: An Exploratory Behavioral Analysis". *Academy of Management Journal,* vol. 19, no. 4, December.

Shannon, C.E., and W. Weaver. 1949. *The Mathematical Theory of Communications,* Urbana, Illinois: University of Illinois Press.

Simon, H.A. 1977. *The New Science of Management Decision.* Third edition. New Jersey: Prentice-Hall.

Stanford Reseach Institute. 1970. "Management Information Systems". Report no. 416, October.

Stoller, D.S., and R.L. Van Horn. 1958. "Design of a Management Information System". *Rand Corporation,* November.

Toffler, Alvin. 1970. *Future Schock.* New York: Random House.

—. *The Third Wave.* New York: William Morrow and Company.

Tou, J.T. 1969. *Advances in Information Systems Science,* vol. 2. New York: Plenum Press.

Vasarhelyi, M.A. 1980. *Cognitive Style Tailored Information Systems.* New York: Graduate School of Business, Columbia University, working paper no. 374A, November.

Voyer, P., and R. Hurtubise. 1979. *Le côté humain des systèmes d'information: une vue pratique* (The Human Side of Information Systems: A Practical View). Monographs on Canadian Public Administration, no. 6. Toronto: Institute of Public Administration of Canada.

Vroom, V.H., and P.W. Yetton. 1973. *Leadership and Decision Making.* Pennsylvania: University of Pittsburgh Press.

Vroom, V.H., and A.G. Jago. 1974. "Decision Making as a Social Process: Normative and Descriptive Models of Leder Behavior". *Decision Science,* vol. 5, no. 4, October.

Weiner, N. 1948. *Cybernetics.* New York: John Wiley and Sons, Inc.

—. 1950. *The Human Use of Human Beings: Cybernetics and Society.* New York: Doubleday.

# Bibliography

Wilkinson, J.W. 1976. "Effective Reporting Structure". *Journal of Systems Management*, November.

Yves, B., S. Hamilton, and G.B. Davis. 1980. "A Framework for Research in Computer-Based Management Information Systems". *Management Science*, vol. 26, no. 9, September.

Yvon, P.J., and C. Semin. 1970. *Comment concevoir un système intégré de gestion* (How to Design an Integrated Information System). Paris: Entreprise Moderne d'Édition.

# INDEX

## A

Ackoff, R.L. 33
action 25
Agence d'ARC xiii
analysis 6
analyst 26
 information systems 44

analytical approach 11
Argyris, C. 90
Athey, T.H. 3
Auerbach Publisher's 119

## B

Bandyopadhyay, R. 123
Blumenthal, S.C. 44, 48, 52
boundary 4
Brainstorming 16, 19-21
Briggs Myers, Y. 101, 104

## C

Carper, W.B. 90
Cartesian method 7, 9
catalyst 73
Churchman, C.W. 105
committee 47
 design 47
 steering 47

communication 29
 theory 29

component 3
Computer Assisted Design (CAD) 69, 124
control 25
criteria, success 14
Critical Path Method (CPM) 19
cybernetics 5

## D

Dalkey, N. 19
data 23
data dictionary 50
data processing 24
de Rosnay, J. 3, 4, 9, 11
decision 25
decision maker 4, 102-104 124
decision-making process 91, 110, 112, 113
Delphi 16, 19, 39
Descartes, R. 7
design 4, 7, 17
documentation, analysis, and design
 form 87, 109, 124
Drucker, P. 105
Dunn's Review 125

## E

Ecole nationale d'administration publique
 (ENAP)  xiv
efficacy  122
efficiency  122
Electronic Data Processing (EDP)  24, 37
energy  23
entropy  23
environment  4
evaluation  30, 32
 reporting system  30, 32

## F

feasibility study  15
feedback  5, 25
 negative  5
 positive  5

Files Consolidation Method  50
framework  59-72, 81-87, 109
 global conceptual  59-72, 81-87, 109

frameworks  54-59, 123
 conceptual design  54-59, 123

Fried, L.  46

## G

globality  4

## H

Helmer, O.  19
hierarchy  4
Horton, F.W.  xiv, 120
human information system  33-35
humanization tools  91-118

## I

information  23-25, 27, 124
 report  65, 73-75, 109, 111
input  25, 73, 109
inquiring systems  90, 105-109, 115,
 116, 145
interface  4

## J

Jago, A.G.  91-97
Jung, C.  98, 100

## L

Lafontaine, R.  105
Landry, M.  9, 10
Leifer, R.  23
Lemoigne, J.L.  16, 23
Lessoil, B.  105
limit  4
link  3
logical classification approaches  52-59, 65,
 76, 79, 87, 109
Lucas, H.C. Jr.  46, 70

## S

scientific method  5, 10
Semin, C.  49, 53
Simon, H.A.  15, 18
simulation  17, 18
St-Exupery, A.  xiii
structurability  73, 76
structure  4
study  48
   preliminary  48
synthesis  6
system  5
   closed  5
   definitions  3
   goal-seeking  33
   open  5
   options  13, 14
   purposeful  33
   state-maintaining  33
systemography  16-18
systems  9, 17, 25
   analysis  9, 17, 25
   approach  6, 10, 11, 24
   automated office  70, 72
   decision support  28
   operational  28
   plan  48
   reporting  28, 30, 117
   theory  5, 6

## T

Toffler, A.  5, 36-38, 132
top management  25

## V

visual representation panel  50
von Bertalanffy, L.  5, 6
Vroom, V.H.  91-97

## W

weighting factor  12

## Y

Yetton, P.W.  91-97
Yvon, P.  49, 53